Julio de Santa Ana / Good News to the Poor

Julio de Santa Ana

Good News to the Poor

The Challenge of the Poor
in the History of the Church

ORBIS BOOKS

Maryknoll, New York 10545

1979

Second Printing

The Catholic Foreign Mission Society of America (Maryknoll) recruits and trains people for overseas missionary service. Through Orbis Books Maryknoll aims to foster the international dialogue that is essential to mission. The books published, however, reflect the opinions of their author and are not meant to represent the official position of the society.

Library of Congress Cataloging in Publication Data

Santa Ana, Julio de.
    Good news to the poor.

    Part of a study undertaken by the Commission on the Churches' Participation in Development, World Council of Churches.
    Reprint of the ed. published by the CCPD, Geneva.
    Includes index.
    1. Church and the poor—History. 2. Poor—
Biblical teaching. I. World Council of Churches.
Commission on the Churches' Participation in
Development. II. Title.
BV639.P6S2713   1979   261.8'34'41   78-18763
ISBN 0-88344-158-6 pbk.

Translated from the Spanish by Helen Whittle

First published by the Commission on the Churches' Participation in Development of the World Council of Churches, copyright © 1977 by World Council of Churches, Geneva

U.S. edition, 1979, by Orbis Books, Maryknoll, New York 10545, typeset in Switzerland and printed in the United States of America

See, Yahweh is enthroned for ever,
He sets up his throne for judgment;
He is going to judge the world with justice,
and pronounce a true verdict on the nations.

May Yahweh be a stronghold for the oppressed,
a stronghold when times are hard.
Those who acknowledge your name can rely on you;
you never desert those who seek you, Yahweh.

To Yahweh with his home in Zion, sing praise,
tell the nations of his mighty actions;
He, the avenger of blood, remembers them,
He does not ignore the cry of the wretched.

(Psalm 9 : 7-12)

HOW HAPPY ARE YOU WHO ARE POOR:
YOURS IS THE KINGDOM OF GOD.

(Luke 6 : 20)

Contents

Introduction

Poverty and affluence are two striking realities of our time. On the one side, half the human family lives in poverty, the majority of them in absolute poverty. Their number is increasing day by day. Their situation is deteriorating. Their very survival is under constant threat. On the other side, there is another quarter of the world's population living in unprecedented affluence. Their standard of life is steadily increasing. This contradictory situation is fraught with many problems and serious challenges. The widening gulf between the rich and poor is an obvious challenge. The plight of the millions of poor people and their struggle for survival is another cause for alarm. So is the affluence of the rich which is part of the cause of the sufferings of the poor. The increasing demands of the affluent on the scarce resources of the earth pose a threat both to the environment and to future generations. It is doubtful whether affluence has brought a better quality of life for even the present generation. The predicament of the proverbial camel trying to get through the eye of the needle applies equally to the rich individuals and to the affluent societies.

The problem of poverty is nothing new. Neither is the question of the rich and their wealth. Almost all societies throughout history had both rich and poor. What is new is the unprecedented increase in the world's wealth, the emergence of affluent nations and their links with the poor societies in a world fast shrinking into a neighbourhood. In other words, the age-old issue of the rich and the poor has acquired global dimensions. Besides, the present plight of the poor and certain trends in the affluent societies are so serious that they need to be tackled with apocalyptic urgency.

There is no doubt about the increasing awareness of these challenging facts among the churches. The Fifth Assembly of the World

Council of Churches at Nairobi was unanimous in acknowledging
the gravity of the situation. Many groups of Christians around the
world are engaged in various types of responses. In order to facilitate
the growing awareness among churches and accelerate the process
of Christian responses, the Commission on the Churches' Participation in Development (CCPD) has been engaged in a number of
action/reflection programmes. As part of these efforts, the Commission decided to undertake a study on "The Church and the Poor".
Since the poor and the rich are correlative terms, the study is as much
about the Church and the rich as it is about the Church and the poor.
It is intended to draw out some of the lessons from the Christian
heritage to inform and inspire attitudes and actions relevant to the
contemporary challenges.

The study on "The Church and the Poor" is envisaged in three
parts. The first part deals with insights and perspectives on the
issue from the Bible and from the history of the Church, from its
early period through the Middle Ages. The second volume will be
a symposium of essays presenting the different perspectives and
lessons emerging from the history of the churches from the time of
the Industrial Revolution to the present period. A third volume
will discuss how the problem is posed in our time and the way the
churches perceive the issue and respond to it.

This volume, entitled: "Good News to the Poor", is the first of
the three parts of the study mentioned above. The first three chapters
present some of the major insights emerging from the Bible. The
next two deal with the early period of church history. As the conversion of King Constantine to the Christian faith was an historic event
which introduced new trends of thought and practice, this period is
examined in the sixth chapter. After that, the reader is invited to
look at certain interesting developments in the western churches
in the late Middle Ages. As the theological thinking and practices
of the churches, though sociologically conditioned, are based fundamentally on the Bible, biblical interpretations form the main thread
throughout this volume. The last chapter is a summary of the main
biblical insights and lessons from history and their relevance for
our time.

This volume does not pretend to be a comprehensive presentation
of biblical insights or ecclesial experiences through the centuries.
For example, no attempt is made to look at the major part of the
Middle Ages. More importantly, the lessons from the history of the

eastern churches have hardly been dealt with. It is our hope that this latter omission will be made up in the subsequent two volumes.

The author of this volume, Dr Julio de Santa Ana, is a member of the CCPD staff. Before coming to Geneva in 1972, he served the Church and Society movement in Latin America (ISAL). He studied both theology and sociology in Argentina and France, and is a member of the Methodist Church in Uruguay. CCPD is grateful to Dr de Santa Ana for finding time in the midst of his many programme activities to prepare this volume. We are fortunate in having in him a person who "does" theology, that is, theology done in and for social practice.

The purpose of this volume is to facilitate a process of ecumenical reflection on the teachings of the Bible and the lessons from church history on the challenge of the poor. Such reflection, if it does not lead and is not related to actual practice, may remain academic and sterile. In that sense, we hope this volume will be used as a tool for development education and as resource material for social action for justice. CCPD would appreciate learning from the readers their comments and reactions as well as the ways in which they make use of this publication.

C. I. ITTY
Director
Commission on the Churches'
Participation in Development

Acknowledgements

To Commissioners, staff and friends of the Commission on the Churches' Participation in Development of the World Council of Churches for their numerous suggestions and ideas.

To Mrs Helen Whittle for translating and editing the manuscript from the Spanish.

To Mr Victor Koilpillai for his assistance in giving the book its final form.

To Miss Angela Horton for attending to production details and seeing it through the press.

1 · The Poor and Poverty in the Old Testament

The Old Testament vocabulary

The language of the Old Testament is very precise; the texts speak much more frequently of the poor than of poverty.[1] But the Old Testament perspective on poverty is not always clear. For example, in the Wisdom literature of Israel (which in part reflects elements of the wisdom of other peoples), poverty is sometimes seen as the result of laziness (Prov. 6 : 6-11; 10 : 4; 20 : 4-13; 24 : 30-34), the product of idle chatter (Prov. 14 : 23), or as resulting from worthless pursuits (Prov. 28 : 19, see also 12 : 11), or the search for pleasure (Prov. 21 : 17; 23 : 20-21, etc.). As with almost all the expressions in Wisdom literature (not only that of Israel, but of almost all the peoples of history), they reflect observations on human experience which could easily be made today. Their value lies in the exhortation to work and a serious and earnest approach to life. Clearly, however, they cannot be applied to all types of poverty, so there are many cases where they will not be of great help in the fight to eradicate it. On the other hand, the Wisdom literature also includes affirmations which have a concrete historical meaning. These are the cases where a severe judgment is passed on "a poor man swollen with pride, a rich man who is a liar, and an adulterous old man who has no sense" (Ecclus. 25 : 2). In other words, those who, being of a humble state, do not accept this fact and try to hide it by puffing themselves up with pride are not respectable; neither are those who use trickery and fraud in their business dealings, nor adulterous and debauched old people. This would indicate that poverty need not be hidden; there is no reason to be ashamed of it.

However, some Old Testament passages point out that, just as human wellbeing is a divine blessing, poverty sometimes implies a punishment from God. It is one of the threats used against those who transgress the laws (Deut. 28 : 15-46; Lev. 26 : 14-26), or which the prophets address to the evildoers (Isa. 3 : 16-24; 14 : 1; 5 : 9-10), and which the oppressed also direct towards those who accuse them (Ps. 109 : 10-12). The wise give the form of a doctrinal sentence to this judgment (Prov. 13 : 18, 21, 25; cf. also what Job's friends said: 5 : 1-7; 15 : 26-35; 20; 22; 27 : 13-23). As Fr A. George says: "There are some valid elements in these positions: the meaning of the values of this world, and, above all, deep faith in the justice of God. Their weakness lies in thinking of God's justice only in the narrow framework of worldly punishment, owing to ignorance of the transcendental destiny which God assigned to his people." And he adds: "Pagan and biblical wisdom were able to detect the drawbacks of this solution and to see poverty as a scandal." [2]

We could say, then, in the Old Testament poverty is considered an evil, as a constant and painful fact, whose consequences are the establishment of relationships of dependence and oppression which lead to the false elevation of the powerful (false because it is not in accord with the true will of God) and to the humiliation of the helpless. In this perspective, poverty and misery are seen as abnormal. The believer strives to correct them; if he is poor, he tries to do this through prayer; those who seek to help the poor do so through neighbourly assistance. Hence, the requirement to help the poor, the widow and the orphan (Ex. 21 : 1-11; 22 : 20-23, etc.).

If poverty is regarded in this light, how does the Old Testament regard wealth? First of all, the goods of this world seem to be considered as nourishment which God gives to his people to allow them to satisfy the needs of the least privileged in society (if they are truly hungry and thirsty), rather than possessions which are to be accumulated. This is the meaning of the story in Exodus 16. (See especially v. 18 which is echoed by St Paul in II Cor. 8 : 15.) Thus, the satisfaction of real needs is acceptable, but the unnecessary accumulation of goods is severely judged. For example, the decadence of the kingdom of Solomon is understood by some as resulting from the policy of accumulating riches carried out at that time by the central power in Israel and further accentuated by Solomon's successor (I Kings 12). In the view of the Old Testament, avarice and the accumulation of goods constitute a challenge to the lordship of God, and in this sense indicate a lack of faith and trust in him. As Fr George points out in the work quoted above, "The faithful of Yahweh consider above all that wealth is often linked with injustice. The oppressors of the poor who are denounced by the prophets are presumably rich, although the prophets do not identify them as such (the identification of the "rich" as "wicked" comes only in Isa. 53 : 9). It was, above all, the wisdom writers who sought to analyse how wealth leads to sin: these writers denounce wealth as the source of pride (Prov. 28 : 11), unbelief (Prov. 30 : 9), and, more precisely, false security based on worldly goods which turns men away from trust in God (Ps. 52 : 9; Prov. 11 : 28; Job 31 : 24, etc.). These experiences and judgments do not constitute a condemnation or rejection of wealth, although they call for a sense of proportion as to its value and moderation in its use (Prov. 30 : 7-9; Eccles. 5 : 17-19, etc.)." [3]

Much more important than any accumulated wealth is the knowledge of God, which shows itself in a just attitude to the cause of the needy and afflicted. As Jeremiah said to Jehoiakim: "Woe to him who builds his house by unrighteousness, and his upper rooms by injustice; who makes his neighbour serve him for nothing, and does not give him his wages; who says, 'I will build myself a great house with spacious upper rooms', and cuts out windows for it, paneling it with cedar, and painting it with vermillion. Do you think you are a king, because you compete in cedar? Did not your father eat and drink and do justice and righteousness? Then it was well with him. He judged the cause of the poor and needy; then it was well. Is not this to know me?, says the Lord." (Jer. 22 : 13-16) [4] According to these words of the prophet, he who accumulates wealth beyond his needs and to the detriment of others does not know God. His injustice is contrary to divine righteousness.

This helps us to define more precisely the meaning of "poor" in the Old Testament. The poor being dependent can also mean dependence on God. It is in this sense that the evangelist, Matthew, was to include in the beatitudes the "poor in spirit", while Luke speaks only of "the poor" as blessed. The "poor in spirit" are those who depend totally on God, who trust only in the Lord. But, the poor man is also — and perhaps this is the most important thing — a slave to others, he is in a subordinate position, and for this reason, if he recevies anything, it is not because he demands it, but because he asks humbly for it, in the form of a supplication (Deut. 24 : 14-15; Ps. 22 : 69). Later, this notion of being poor took on a spiritual dimension, until it came to mean someone who is like a slave before God, obeying him as a servant obeys his master (Ps. 25 : 9; 34 : 2-3), bowing completely to his will (Ps. 25 : 15).

The prophetic message on the fact of poverty and the existence of the poor

Concern for the condition of the poor had already appeared in the Middle East before the writing of the books of the Old Testament began. However, the Old Testament reinforced the defence lines of the poor and helpless. The duty to help the poor was already established in the law of the Covenant, before the time of the Kings; this law takes up the defence of the slave (Ex. 21 : 1-11; 21 : 26-27), the widow and the orphan (22 : 20-23), the servant who is loaned money (22 : 25), the innocent beggar who has had proceedings begun against him and who must be protected during the year of release (Ex. 23 : 6, 11). All this had already been implied earlier in the laws of Israel's neighbours. However, the Mosaic covenant "gives them a new meaning: the inferior condition of the poor and humble is felt as an atttack on the solidarity of the people of God. The Lord of the Covenant pays special attention to the disinherited of his people. It is in this perspective of the Covenant that the eighth-century prophets take up the defence of the poor, victims of the social crisis of their time... They thus denounce all forms of oppression which are implicit in economic growth: taxes and suffocating tithes (Amos 4 : 1; 5 : 11-12; Isa. 3 : 14-15), fraudulent trade (Amos 8 : 4-5), the seizure of land (Micah 2 : 1-3), the selling as slaves of those who cannot pay their debts (Amos 2 : 6; 8 : 6), unjust judgments (Amos 5 : 12; Isa. 10 : 1-2; 32 : 7; Jer. 5 : 28; 22 : 16), the implicit violence of the injustice of the oppressor (Ezek. 16 : 49; 18 : 12-13; Zech. 7 : 10).

"In contrast to this, Isaiah reintroduces in his picture of the Messiah king the old ideology of the king who protects the poor (Isa. 11 : 4); a century later, Jeremiah is to show that this ideal was realized in Josiah, thus condemning the abuses of Jehoiakim (Jer. 22 : 15-16). Under the influence of the first prophets, Deuteronomy developed the prescriptions of the Law of the Covenant in favour of the poor. This is particularly clear in the laws concerning the tithe (Deut. 14 : 29; 26 : 12-13), the year of release (Deut. 15 : 1-11), the slave (15 : 12-18), the feasts (16 : 11, 14), the protection of the weakest (24 : 10-21; 27 : 19).

"This same concern for the poor is again found in the law of holiness (Lev. 19 : 9, 10, 13; 23 : 22), in the Psalms (41 : 2; 82 : 3-4; 109 : 16; 112 : 9). In the Wisdom literature, there is often an exhortation to help the poor, be it in the old wisdom style (Prov. 21 : 13;

31 : 21; the theme of the king who protects the poor is found in Prov. 29 : 14 and 31 : 8-9), but also with an explicitly religious motivation (Prov. 14 : 21, 31´; 17 : 5; 19 : 17; 22 : 23; 28 : 27; 29 : 7; Job 29 : 12-16; 30 : 24-25; 31 : 16-23, etc.)." [5]

The prophets denounce poverty as an evil — the result of the injustice of the powerful. They look for a just society, for which their inspiration comes from the remembrance of the Mosaic ideal experienced in the Exodus period, when the nation of Israel was taking shape. According to their judgment, the acceptance of poverty and the injustice which generates it is a return to a situation of slavery, similar to the period spent under the Egyptian yoke (Deut. 5 : 15; 16 : 22; Lev. 26 : 13). For this reason, the prophets, in denouncing poverty, also denounce the causes which produce it and those who profit from it (Amos 5 : 7; Jer. 5 : 28). In other words, they refer not only to particular situations (see above), but also to those who are responsible for them.[6] By this, the prophets also imply that poverty is not the result of fate or blind destiny. Basically, they see it as the result of the behaviour of those whom they have denounced because of the injustice of their actions. "Thus says the Lord : 'For three transgressions of Israel, and for four, I will not revoke the punishment; because they sell the righteous for silver, and the needy for a pair of shoes — they that trample the head of the poor into the dust of the earth, and turn aside the way of the afflicted'. . ." (Amos 2 : 6-7). The message is clear: people are in misery because they are the victims of the injustice of others. "Woe to those who decree iniquitous decrees, and the writers who keep writing oppression, to turn aside the needy from justice and to rob the poor of my people of their right, that widows may be their spoil, and that they may make the fatherless their prey!" (Isa. 10 : 1-2).

It was following this line of the prophets that the later books of the Old Testament gave the means of assisting the poor the term *Sedaqa*, that is, to do justice, to fulfil the will of God, and which the LXX was to translate as *elemosyne* (hence our term "alms"). But with this we move on to the forms of struggle against poverty in the Old Testament.

Efforts to overcome poverty in the Old Testament

Some people do not appreciate the true value of the prophetic message; they even claim that it constitutes only a denunciation, a criticism, and that therefore it has no positive value. They fail to see that any criticism contains a positive element in that it enables its audience to understand what must be changed. This positive aspect is accentuated by the fact that the prophetic message includes not only a denunciation but also the announcement of what God seeks to carry out in history. There were those who, on the basis of this announcement, sought to shape and bring about continuous reforms in the life of the people of Israel, through which they hoped to strike at the very roots of poverty; the injustice of some sectors against others.

As Gustavo Gutierrez points out: "The Bible speaks of positive and concrete measures to prevent poverty from becoming established among the people of God. In Leviticus and Deuteronomy, there is very detailed legislation designed to prevent the accumulation of wealth and the consequent exploitation. It is said, for example, that what remains in the fields after the harvest and the gathering of olives and grapes should not be collected; it is for the alien, the orphan, and the widow (Deut. 24 : 19-21; Lev. 19 : 9-10). Even more, the fields should not be harvested to the very edge so that something remains for the poor and the aliens (Lev. 23 : 22). The Sabbath, the day of the Lord, has a social significance; it is a day of rest for the slave and the alien (Ex. 23 : 12; Deut. 5 : 14). The triennial tithe is not to be carried to the temple; rather it is for the alien, the orphan and the widow (Deut. 14 : 28-29; 26 : 12). Interest on loans is forbidden (Ex. 22 : 25; Lev. 25 : 35-37; Deut. 23 : 20). Other important measures include the Sabbath year and the jubilee year. Every seven years, the fields will be left to lie fallow 'to provide food for the poor of your people' (Ex. 23 : 11; Lev. 25 : 2-7), although it is recognized that this duty is not always fulfilled (Lev. 26 : 34-35). After seven years, the slaves were to regain their freedom (Ex. 21 : 2-6), and debts were to be pardoned (Deut. 15 : 1-18). This is also the meaning of the jubilee year of Lev. 25 : 10 ff. It was... a general emancipation... of all the inhabitants of the land. The fields lay fallow; every man re-entered his ancestral property, i.e. the fields and houses which had been alienated returned to their original owners." [7]

This struggle to eradicate poverty makes it clear that it is not a matter of explaining how things come about (that is, how the cosmos is ordered, how the laws of nature are fulfilled, and so on), but of being open to history and, through participation in it, to the action of God which continually intervenes in history and which again and again comes to men with its message. The struggle for justice for the people of Israel can only be explained in the context of God's action to correct the injustices of men and to make his righteousness triumphant. To seek to eradicate poverty is to try to be faithful to the God who is awaited and who is coming to us.[8] Now, it is clear from the experiences of Israel throughout its history, and of other people who have attempted with varying degrees of success to overcome poverty, that those who undertake this in a spirit of hope and openness to the future are precisely those who have had practical experience of what it means to be poor. It was this experience, at both the material and social levels, which seems to have led the men and women of Israel to adopt an attitude of humble submission to God and of trust in his grace. "Strictly speaking, this is not an idealization of poverty, since it never had any value in itself for the faithful in the Old Testament. However, we must recognize that poverty for them had an unquestionable religious significance; it called them to open themselves to God and prepared them to receive the demands and the gift of Jesus." [9]

Being poor: condition for the practice of true piety

What we have said so far about the condition of poverty and of the poor in the Old Testament helps us to see how, on the basis of this understanding and with the passage of time, a new line of thought took shape in Israel concerning poverty. It can be considered as giving a spiritual value to the fact of being poor on the basis of the previous experiences of the people of God. Basically, and continuing an idea hinted at in the previous paragraph, the poor were also understood as those who waited for Yahweh. According to A. Gelin,[10] the poor are those who live in an attitude of *spiritual infancy*, and so are open to receiving everything from God, in complete humility before the Lord. This new direction can already be detected in the prophetic message of Zephaniah (Zeph. 2 : 3); from this point, those who await anxiously and meekly the liberating action of the Messiah are called "poor", and this constitutes the basis for the existence of the "faithful remnant" ("those who are left in Israel") of the people of God (Zeph. 3 : 12-13). Faithfulness to the Lord means waiting for his coming in *humility and poverty*. The "poor of Yahweh" is the man who is ready to suffer and be persecuted because of his faithfulness to the Lord,[11] as is the case of Simeon and Anna narrated in St Luke's gospel (2 : 32-38). They are typical figures of "the poor of Yahweh" in the Scriptures.

All this raises the question of the significance of humility in the Old Testament. Once more, we must turn to Zephaniah, the only prophet who requires that meek submission to the will of God *('anâwâ)* be practised along with justice (Zeph. 2 : 3). For Zephaniah, humility is the source of justice; only the meek are able to wait faithfully for the signs of the saving justice of God.

Jeremiah, in persecution and later in freedom, praises the Lord "for He has delivered the life of the needy *('èbyôn)* from the hand of evildoers" (Jer. 20 : 13). In this passage, the prophet does not appear as a destitute, but as a persecuted man who calls on the good will of God towards the victims of injustice. Apparently, Fr George is right in saying that, in this way, Jeremiah indirectly proclaims that his weakness and humility have been the sources of his salvation".[12] This attitude can also be seen among many writers of the Psalms who appear as "poor"; many had dramatic experience of poverty: they were sick, oppressed, imprisoned, humiliated, threatened. However, they almost always express their acceptance of this unfortunate experience until the Lord sees fit to free them. In this sense, the book of Psalms can be seen as the one through which the poor of Israel expressed themselves. "Because they have nothing, because they are despised and slandered, they await the manifestation of the Lord's judgment" (Ps. 58 : 11-12), and the justice which they know can only come from God (Ps. 40 : 17; 109 : 31; 69 : 34). They are the ones who, the New Testament tells us, awaited "the consolation of Israel" (Luke 2 : 25). It was among these poor that the Messianic hope was particularly vigorous (Luke 1 : 51-53; 2 : 8-14; 2 : 25-38). Whatever the nature of their needs, often very worldly, they were still the most ready to receive Christ." [13]

Since wealth and poverty are relative terms, we can then contrast the poor with the rich according to this line of thought. The rich man is self-sufficient; he has accumulated wealth in such a way that he believes he no longer need fear God. In contrast, the poor are the pious who have no worldly goods to support them, nor any worldly influence to count on. In the absence of goods and influence, in their search to be faithful to the Lord, they relate their whole existence to God, directing all their life towards him and looking to him as the only source of their "salvation". Clearly, at the time when this view of poverty was taking shape, being "poor" was understood principally from the religious, spiritual perspective, which did not necessarily include the economic aspects of poverty.[14] However, these "poor of Yahweh", whether or not they lived in misery, were particularly sensitive to the existence of physical poverty and injustice. Hence their prayers, some of which have been recorded in the book of Psalms. Faced with the scandal of poverty, while ready to act against it, the "poor of Yahweh" first address themselves to God through prayer, for only from the Lord can they hope for the fulfilment of his aspirations.[15]

The figure of Job also reflects this attitude. In the book of Job, we meet a theme which also appears in some passages in the Psalms, for example 73 : 23-28: "Nevertheless, I am continually with thee: thou dost hold my right hand. Thou dost guide me with thy counsel, and afterward thou wilt receive me to glory. Whom have I in heaven but thee? And there is nothing upon earth that I desire besides thee. My flesh and my heart may fail, but God is the strength of my heart and my portion for ever. For lo, those who are far from thee shall perish; thou dost put an end to those who are false to thee. But for me, it is good to be near God; I have made the Lord God my refuge, that I may tell of all thy works." This shows submission to the unfathomable decrees of God. "Such acquiescence may go together with a confidence that God will redress the situation in the future, particularly if man is content to renounce his self-will and wait quietly upon him. Thus, there grows up a *unique conception of faith*. To believe in God is not simply to believe in his existence, but meekly to submit to his will and wait upon him in quietness and confidence."[16]

If we read through the Psalms again, we can be more definite about this religious attitude of the "poor of Yahweh" which appears in Israel after the return from exile. The poor and oppressed who seek the Lord know the divine strength (Ps. 9 : 11; 34 : 11). Their attitude towards God is to abandon their will and accept his purposes (Ps. 10 : 14; 34 : 9; 37 : 40). Rather than fearing the powerful of this world, they must fear the Lord (Ps. 25 : 12-14; 34 : 8-10). Is it by observing his commandments that the poor become whole, righteous and just (Ps. 34 : 16, 20, 22; 37 : 17-18)? So the "poor of Yahweh" are the friends of God. The enemies of God are the proud, who appear as contradictory figures to the poor and the destitute. The highest expression of this kind of piety is found in the beatitudes of Jesus, pronounced centuries after this spiritual attitude towards poverty was defined.

In concluding this chapter, it should be said that a little more than a century before the birth of Jesus, the Qumran community included some who defined themselves consciously as *ebyonim*, and even became known as "the community of the *ebyonim*".[17] By this, they did not mean that they had rejected the use of money, nor renounced money, although they sought to practise community ownership of goods in a style which was a forerunner to what happened later in the primitive Christian community of Jerusalem (cf. Acts 2 : 42-45; 4 : 32-34). In defining themselves as poor, as beggars, they made known their awareness of being persecuted and rejected; nevertheless, their firm intention was to submit meekly to the demands of the Lord in whom they had put their faith.

NOTES:

[1] A. GEORGE: "La Pauvreté dans l'Ancien Testament" in *La Pauvreté Evangé-lique*, pp. 14-18. Paris: Ed. du Cerf, 1971. Fr George, who has made a careful study of the subject, says that "The poor are mentioned about 245 times by six main terms which are almost always rendered in modern translations by "poor". "*'Anî*" and "*'ânâw*" must be taken together as they refer to the same root and are often confused by copyists. The meaning of the original root is still the subject of dicussion; most believe it denotes the act of "inclining oneself" or "to be inclined"; A. Rahlfs defines it as "adopting the stance of a servant before his master"; H. Birkeland suggests "to be weak, small, unimportant", "having less strength and less value", but E. Baumel prefers "being in the situation of having to respond". Be that as it may, the term describes a situation of social inferiority. This accords with the use of these terms, which the texts often apply to the oppressed. "*'Anî*" appears 80 times. It refers to one who bows down, who gives in, who submits. The LXX translate it by "*ptôchos*" (38 times), "*pénês*" and "*pénichros*" (13 times), "*tapeinos*" (9 times) and "*praüs*" (4 times), while the translators of the Jerusalem Bible translate it variously by "poor", "miserable", "unfortunate", "afflicted", "humble".
    "*'Anâw*" is used 25 times, always in the plural except for Num. 12 : 3. At times, it tends to mean not only the humble and oppressed, but also the humble and the meek (but did the primitive text say "*âni*" or "*'ânâw*"?): thus the LXX translate it by "*praüs*" (8 times), "*tapeinos*" (6 times), "*pénês*" (4 times), "*ptôchos*" (4 times), while the Jerusalem Bible translates it 5 times by "poor", twice by "unfortunate", and 15 times by "humble". Probably the moral and religious significance of the term has (been) heightened with time. The word "*'èbyon*" is found 61 times in the Hebrew Bible (especially in the Psalms: 24 times). P. Humbert concludes his study of the use of this term by saying that while it refers to the poor..., it also implies an essential idea of pleading. The "*'èbyon*" is both poor and a beggar. The Jerusalem Bible often translates it by "poor", but often by "needy", "unfortunate", "humble".
    "*Dal*" is found 48 times in the Hebrew text: 5 times in the historical books, four in the codes, 13 in the Prophets, 6 in the Psalms, 20 in the Wisdom texts.

The root "*dâlal*" means "without importance", "weak", "frail". The texts use it to denote the weak in the physical or social sense.

"*Râsh*" is used 21 times. It is the participle of the verb "*rûsh*", which means "to be destitute", "needy".

"*Miskén*" is found 4 times. Originally, it seems to indicate "he who depends", "who is subjected" (the needy). This vocabulary expresses an idea of poverty which is quite different from ours. In our modern languages, as well as in Greek and Latin, poverty is the absence of goods: it is an economic notion. Hebrew sometimes denotes it as a lack *("râsh")* or a plea *("'èbyon")*, but above all it sees it as a situation of dependence *("'âni"*, *"'ânâw"*, *"miskén")* or weakness *("dal")*. To the men of the Bible, the poor are not so much needy as inferior, small, oppressed: it is a social notion. So, when the poor seek to see their social condition in spiritual terms, they do not idealize indifference to the goods of this world, but rather voluntary and loving submission to the will of God.

2 *Ibid.*, pp. 22-23.

3 *Ibid.*, p. 29.

4 Cf. RUDOLF BULTMANN: *Primitive Christianity*, p. 22 ff. New York: Meridian Books (tr. R. H. Fuller), 1956.

5 A. GEORGE: *op. cit.*, pp. 24-25.

6 GUSTAVO GUTIERREZ: *A Theology of Liberation*, p. 293 ff. Maryknoll, New York: Orbis Books, 1973.

7 *Ibid.*, p. 360.

8 Cf. RUDOLF BULTMANN: *op. cit.*, p. 34. "In both cases — individual and national — there is no idea of order and purpose in the universe. Instead, there is a future to be inaugurated by God. That is the Old Testament answer to the problem of theodicy, insofar as there is any answer at all. God confronts man with his blessing and demand, judging him in each successive moment. Every such moment, however, points towards the future. God is always a God who comes."

9 A. GEORGE: *op. cit.*, p. 32.

10 A. GELIN: *Les Pauvres de Jahvé*, p. 29. Paris: Ed. du Cerf, 1953.

11 JEAN COLSON: *Le Sacerdoce du Pauvre*, p. 50. Paris: Ed. SOS, 1971. Cf. also: R. LAURENTIN: *Commentaire à Luc I-II*, pp. 114-115. Paris: Ed. Gabalda, 1957.

12 A. GEORGE: *op. cit.*, p. 31.

13 A. PÉRY: article "Pauvre", in *Vocabulaire Biblique*, p. 222. Neuchâtel and Paris: Delachaux et Niestlé, 2nd edition, 1956.

14 A. SEIDENSTICKER: "St Paul et la Pauvreté" in *La Pauvreté Evangélique, op. cit.*, p. 95.

15 A good example of this is the prayer of the humiliated Anna in I Samuel 1 : 9-20. Many terms in this prayer appear in the song of Mary commonly known as *The Magnificat* (Luke 1 : 46-55).

16 Cf. RUDOLF BULTMANN: *op. cit.*, p. 32.

17 Quoted by A. GEORGE: *op. cit.*, p. 32.

2 · The Poor and Poverty in the Message of Jesus

At the end of the last chapter, we said that the idea of the "poor of Yahweh" was taking shape in Israelite society in the years preceding the birth of Jesus. This came about through the experiences of the Qumran and Essene communities. According to the writings of Flavius Josephus and Philo of Alexandria, the Essenes practised a life of extreme sobriety and the common ownership of goods. The Qumran manuscripts are not explicit in this respect, but the hymns in them indicate that the community was part of "the poor" living in exile, faithful to God, persecuted by their religious adversaries. The Essenes were organized around the hope of God's intervention in history. One of the group's basic characteristics was indifference to worldly goods. "Its originality lay not only in its location in the desert, its pre-monastic structure, its ascetic and mystic doctrine which sought perfection, but rather in the radical nature of the demands it made on its members. From beginning to end, they maintained an attitude of anxious and active readiness for the avenging and saving act of triumphant eschatology." [1]

A direct forerunner of Jesus who was known for this attitude was John the Baptist, whose life and thought are important in our study of the challenge of the poor and poverty to the community of faith. In contrast to the Qumran followers, who settled around the south banks of the Dead Sea, John preached the baptism of repentance for the remission of sins in the Jordan region. The fact that he came to proclaim a message indicates another difference from the Qumran group, whose members did not preach, but always lived in closed communities. According to St Luke (3 : 3-6), John the Baptist was noted for his use of the prophetic words of Isaiah (Isa. 40 : 3-5), which announced salvation "to all flesh". One of the demands of the baptism of repentance preached by John was the acceptance of humility as a preparation for receiving the Messiah who was to come. Only the meek, the poor, the rejected, who experienced the tearing pain of death, could receive the "Servant of Yahweh". So, when John sent messengers from prison to ask Jesus if he was "He who was to come", the Nazarene's answer was to describe the events which confirmed that He was the Son of God: "The blind receive their sight and the lame walk, the lepers are cleansed and the deaf hear, the dead are raised up, *and the poor have good news preached to them*." (Matt. 11 : 5.)

Jesus proclaimed the Kingdom to the poor
In this text from Matthew, Jesus indicates the great importance of the poor in the development of his ministry: it is to them that the Kingdom of God is announced. Even clearer than his response to John is the text with which Jesus begins his public ministry in the Nazareth synagogue, in which He used the words of the prophet Isaiah (61 : 1-2), saying that it is to the poor that the good news is preached: "The Spirit of the Lord is upon me, because he has anointed me to preach good news to the poor. He has sent me to proclaim release to the captives, to recover sight to the blind, to set at liberty those who are oppressed, to proclaim the acceptable year of the Lord." (Luke 4 : 17-19.) This text emphasized what we might call the *privilege of the poor*. In adding after this passage from Isaiah, "Today this scripture has been fulfilled in your hearing" (Luke 4 : 21), Jesus identifies himself as the messenger proclaimed by the prophet and, at the same time, explains that his mission is addressed to the unfortunate, the poor, to whom He already announces an end to their sufferings. Their special place is confirmed by the beatitudes (Matt. 5 : 3-11, especially verse 3, and the parallel passage in Luke 6 : 20, where the blessed are the poor in the material, and not only in the spiritual, sense). In these texts Jesus indicates that with his coming the poor will be blessed, "for theirs is the Kingdom of heaven". Because they have nothing, they are particularly ready to open themselves to the saving action of Jesus. "Only the outcast, the publicans, sinners and harlots are ready to repent. Jesus knows that it was to them he was sent (Mark 2 : 17). Those who first said 'No' repent later (Matt. 21 : 28-31). God takes more pleasure in one sinner who repents than in ninety and nine just persons (Luke 15 : 1-10). It is the hungry and those who mourn, those who know they are poor, who receive the promise of salvation (Luke 6 : 20 ff.; Matt. 5 : 3-6)."[2]

This privilege of the poor also inspires them with hope, not only because the end of their suffering is in sight, but because Jesus' proclamation of the Kingdom also implies the announcement that the judgment of God is at hand. He will reinstate the paths of justice, and restore the damage done to human and social relationships by sin.[3] It is as if He said to the poor: "Behold, God offers you consolation for all ages." In this, the justice of God will appear, for his love will veil and overcome man's sin (Isa. 1 : 16-18), opening the paths of history to a time when justice and responsibility for others will be clearly seen in society. "Here we have the Kingdom whose coming Jesus proclaims: this is precisely the good news which is announced especially to the poor. If we are to understand how this good news concerns the poor in particular, we must take into account the images evoked by this idea of the Kingdom of God. It cannot be separated from the ideal of the royal dignity which Israel is to share with the peoples of the old Near East. From the third millennium before Christ, in Mesopotamia as well as in Egypt, the main function of the king was to ensure justice for his subjects. In exercising this prerogative, the king must take account of reality: his subjects include the powerful and the weak, the rich and the poor. In the natural order of things, the powerful and rich would always manage to abuse their power to oppress and exploit the weak and the poor who, unable to defend themselves, would gradually founder in misery. It is the king's duty to restore the balance. By virtue of this duty, he is the defender of those who cannot defend themselves; he is the appointed protector of the poor, the widow, the orphan, the oppressed. The 'justice' which he must administer to his subjects will consist in guaranteeing the rights of the weak in face of the powerful, as well as repressing the rich who threaten the rights of the poor."[4]

This kind of image, which would certainly have been evoked by the message of Jesus, filled the hearts of the humble with joy. Hence the effect of Jesus' preaching among the multitudes, and the joy which greeted his arrival in Jerusalem on Palm Sunday when he was acclaimed as "the king who comes in the name of the Lord" (Luke 19 : 37-38).

"Blessed are the poor"

In spite of all this, Jesus calls the poor "blessed", "happy", and surely the fulfilment of the Messianic hope in Jesus must have inspired happiness in them. But is this enough to make them forget the pain and suffering caused by poverty? Does the proclamation of the Kingdom of heaven mean that the conditions of a time in which injustice still prevailed were finally overcome? Of course, we know that this is not so easy, and that despair is the state of mind nearest to hope. However, paradoxically, Jesus called the poor "happy". What did our Lord mean by this? It is an important question, for much depends on its clarification — not only our understanding of how we are to "follow Jesus", but also how the community of believers (the Church) should treat the poor.

For example, a very literal interpretation of the beatitudes implies that those whose material condition is humble are the ones who show us the road which leads to the Kingdom of God. This is only a short step from the acceptance of poverty as a norm. It is claimed, then, that to live a Christian life we must be poor, identifying ourselves with the unfortunate and dispossessed in their style of life. But by introducing this as an obligation, we no longer live in the sphere of the Gospel but under the demands of the law. In this case, the law obliges us to be poor; it says that we must accept the demands of poverty because only thus can we receive the Kingdom of God. But this would mean forgetting that the Gospel is given us through grace, and that, as such, it must be lived freely, without obligations or impositions. It also ignores that if conditions are placed on entering the Kingdom of God, those who receive it will not be those who, as "the poor of Yahweh", live in total openness and availability to God's intervention in their lives and in history. More serious still, the insistence on a life of poverty as an essential requirement for entry into the Kingdom imposes conditions on God, and ignores the fact that, even if the Kingdom is promised to the poor, poverty is still a scandal and a manifestation of evil.

However, there is no reason why we should accept too easily an interpretation of these texts which over-spiritualizes the existence of "the poor". For example, A. Gelin, in his work, *Les Pauvres de Yahvé*, severely criticizes those who think that in the beatitudes Jesus actually blessed certain social classes such as the proletariat, the poor peasantry, the unemployed and underprivileged. In this case, entry into the Kingdom would not even be the result of a voluntary choice, a personal response to the call of Jesus, but a consequence imposed on certain social groups by a given socio-economic situation. Gelin points out that: "No sociological state is canonized by the Gospel; none, as such, is placed in direct relationship with the Kingdom." [5]

Four centuries earlier, Calvin pointed out in terms which converged with those of Gelin, if only stated more radically, that in his opinion Matthew's text expressed Jesus' intention more clearly than did Luke's, since experience has often shown that material poverty is accompanied by great pride, which is not consistent with the humility of one who places all his hope in God. In this case, being poor "in spirit" means a voluntary acceptance of poverty. "By adding this epithet, St Matthew limits the beatitude only to those who have learned to be humble under the discipline of the cross." [6] Calvin, then, emphasizes the spiritual aspect, humility and self-effacement, rather than the destitution of those who, because they are poor, are to be blessed.

However, as J. Dupont points out: "The texts immediately raise an objection to these explanations (especially, we should emphasize, against those of A. Gelin). Together with the poor, they include others who suffer. They add 'those who weep' (that is, those who mourn) and also those 'that hunger now' (Luke 6 : 21). The words of Isaiah quoted in Luke 4 associate the poor with prisoners, the blind and the oppressed. When Jesus sends his answer to John the Baptist He tells him what happens to the blind, the crippled, the lepers, the deaf and even the dead. It is clear, then, that it would be incorrect to understand these terms in a spiritual sense which would be in accordance with what is intended by the word 'poor'. Indeed, Jesus proclaims the good news to those who live in misery and misfortune, and in practice this good news means the end of their suffering. This context, therefore, does not suggest that we should spiritualize the notion of poverty." [7]

Then why are the poor "blessed", if their living conditions show how unfortunate they are ? It seems clear that the text does not call upon us to resign ourselves to the condition of poverty, since later — in the Kingdom — the injustice will be compensated by the grace of God. No, the text calls, not for resignation but for hope, especially if in our reading we bear in mind the prophetic tradition of the people of Israel. "If we believe that the Kingdom of God is a gift which is received in history, and if we believe, as the eschatological promises — so charged with human and historical content — indicate to us, that the Kingdom of God necessarily implies the reestablishment of justice in this world, then we must believe that Christ says that the poor are blessed *because* the Kingdom of God has begun: 'The time has come: the Kingdom of God is upon you;' (Mark 1 : 15).

In other words, the elimination of the exploitation and poverty that prevent the poor from being fully human has begun; a Kingdom of justice which goes even beyond what they could have hoped for has begun. They are blessed because the coming of the Kingdom will put an end to their poverty by creating a world of brotherhood. They are blessed because the Messiah will open the eyes of the blind and will give bread to the hungry. Situated in a prophetic perspective, the text in Luke uses the term 'poor' in the tradition of the first major line of thought we have studied: poverty is an evil and therefore incompatible with the Kingdom of God, which has come in its fullness into history and embraces the totality of human existence." [8]

In this perspective, we can see more clearly the reason for the beatitude: the proclamation of the coming of the Kingdom and its saving justice is to bring happiness to all those who have been living in unhappiness and misfortune, for they are the ones who are to benefit from the new age ushered in by the Kingdom of God. In other words, the reason for the blessing, the privilege of the poor, lies neither in their material circumstances nor in their spiritual disposition, but in the way in which God conceives the exercise of his Kingdom: "Blessed are the poor, not because they are better than others, or better prepared to receive the Kingdom which is to come, but because God seeks to make his Kingdom a tangible manifestation of his justice and love for the poor, the suffering and those who live in misery." [9]

To put this in another way, the happiness of the poor has its theological basis in God himself. Our interpretation will not take into account the development of the concept of "poor" in the history of Israel (which is necessary to an understanding of Jesus' message and his proclamation of the Kingdom), if we seek a basis for the privilege which has been granted to them by God in their moral attitudes, social conditions or spiritual positions. The poverty of those to whom Jesus announces the good news of the Kingdom of God is none other than the poverty which arises from the deprivation which makes the poor the victims of hunger and oppression. *This poverty is not a virtue but an evil* which constitutes a challenge to the justice of the Lord who is King of creation. Consequently, this poverty is not proposed as an ideal for Christians; rather it is the condition of many human beings, and the Creator rebels against it, because it directly challenges the honour due to his creation and his loving purpose for man.

This does not mean that anyone who is poor in material terms will receive this blessing. We must rather emphasize that, according to the Scriptures, material and spiritual poverty are interconnected, the latter being the result of the former, according to what we have said about the process of the faithful towards seeing themselves as "the poor of Yahweh". According to A. Péry, Matthew's and Luke's versions are not contradictory but complementary, expressing "simply this dual character of poverty, which must be at the same time internal and practical. This dual concept can help us to avoid false interpretations: material poverty in itself is no use unless it serves to lead the human being towards God. But on the other hand, the spirit of poverty, spiritual poverty as such, can easily be a sham unless it has its source in true material poverty." [10]

The responsibility of the rich

Since it is not God who is the source of the injustice which produces the poverty of many, we cannot maintain that He decides that some shall be rich and some needy. There is in the world a clear disparity in the distribution of the fruits of human labour and the resources available to our societies, but this cannot be blamed on the divine will. Here the message of Jesus is clear, and it is corroborated by the rest of the New Testament. In fact, with the inequality between rich and poor, those who run the greatest risk of God's judgment are the rich. Hence Jesus' radical demand to the rich man who wanted to follow him, that he should sell his possessions and give the proceeds to the poor (Matt. 19 : 16-22; Mark 10 : 17-22; Luke 13 : 18-27; and also Luke 12 : 33-34), a theme to which we shall return in the next chapter.

But, more than this, the New Testament makes it clear that the idea hinted at in the Old Testament, that worldly goods are a sign of God's favour, is unacceptable. On the contrary, the message of Jesus indicates that it is forbidden to take what belongs to God alone (cf. Luke 15 : 22 ff). The Epistle of James emphasizes that the appropriation of wealth necessarily implies some form of injustice (James 5 : 1-6). Similarly, in I John 3 : 17, we see the incompatibility between the accumulation of the goods of this world and the practice of brotherly love. In I Timothy 6 : 17-19, there is a warning to those whose needs are amply supplied ("the rich") not to store up or accumulate wealth, but to place it at the disposal of the needy. The basic purpose of wealth is to help those who live in misery.

We must not automatically conclude that these texts taken together actually extol poverty. On the contrary, it is not agreeable in the sight of God, and He wants an end to it. Hence the attack on the accumulation of wealth by the rich. The existence of poverty announces their ruin, for they seem to place more trust in the abundance of material possessions than in God. The rich man adores money — Mammon — and his attitude is one of true idolatry which the living God cannot accept.

Christ's presence among the poor

According to the Gospel message, although the poor are granted privileges, they are also the unfortunates who must be helped. They are needy people whom we must assist. No other text makes this so clear and emphatic as the famous passage in Matthew 25 : 31-46, where the Lord describes the nature of the Last Judgment, with which the evangelist concludes the public ministry of Jesus. The all-powerful judge considers the unfortunate (the poor, hungry, naked, homeless, thirsty, prisoners, and others) as his brothers; what has been done to them has also been done to him. If anything else was needed to make us understand the importance of our concern for the poor, this text provides it. But it also warns those who follow Christ to remain alert, so that they may recognize his presence at any moment and serve him by serving the poor. This was and is the true attitude of the "poor of Yahweh", always open to meeting their Lord, even when they least expect him, in the humblest of their neighbours.

Thus St John Chrysostomos said: "The master and creator of the universe says, 'I was hungry and you gave me no food' (Matt. 25 : 42). What heart is so hard that it is not moved by these words? Your Lord is out there, dying of hunger, and you give yourself up to gluttony. And the terrible thing is not only this, but as you give yourself up to gluttony, you calmly despise him, and it is very little He asks of you: a piece of bread to assuage his hunger. He is out there, dying of cold, and you dress yourself in silk and turn your gaze away from him, showing him no compassion, but go on your way without mercy. What pardon can such action merit? Then let us not devote our efforts to accumulating wealth at all cost. Let us also consider the way of administering it properly and helping the needy; and let us not exaggerate in the goods which remain and cannot be transferred. This is why the Lord has hidden the last day from us; He wants us to remain alert and vigilant, to encourage us to virtue: 'Watch, therefore, for you know neither the day nor the hour.' (Matt. 25 : 13)." [11]

The meaning of Christ's presence among the poor has a clear eschatological dimension. It does not mean that poverty is sanctified as a virtue, but rather that, while there are poor people, his judgment is still to come. We must, therefore, be ready to accept his will, which is not only for the last day since what we do or do not do today to recognize his presence among the poor is already something the Judge will take into account in his judgment. This is of vital importance to the Church which, in the light of Matt. 25 : 31-46, defines its faithfulness to Jesus Christ in accordance with its position in relation to the challenge of the poor and poverty, and also according to the relationship of the poor to them. José Míguez Bonino, at the consultation organized by the Commission on Inter-Church Aid, Refugee and World Service (CICARWS) and the Commission on the Churches' Participation in Development (CCPD) on "Justice and Development" (Montreux, December 1974), emphasized the importance of the implications of this text to the life of the Christian community, because in the end it is a matter of how to be faithful to Jesus Christ as a people who confess him as Lord and try to follow in his paths. The Argentine theologian put it in this way: "No one will question that the Church has to concern itself with the poor. But should we say more than this? I want to introduce this subject by referring to a book by a French Dominican who worked for several years in Uruguay, Benoit Dumas, and who has written a very interesting book entitled, *The Two Alienated Faces of the One Church*. His basic thesis is that the poor belong to the understanding of the mystery of the Church, or, if you wish to use another language, that the poor belong to the understanding of the very nature of the Church. He says that if the identity of the Church is found in Jesus Christ, *ubi Christus ibi ecclesia*, then we must pay attention to the fact that Christ said that He would be present when his words were remembered and the meal was shared, and that He would be present in the poor and the oppressed. Fr Dumas uses, of course, Matthew 25 as the basic text. I will not fight here for a sacramental interpretation because I do not think that his point rests on the interpretation of this text. You may refer to many other texts throughout the Bible. I think that the point he establishes is valid in any case. And therefore he says, in our present situation as churches, the Church does not recognize itself in the poor. It may recognize the poor as a very important part of the world, but the Church does not recognize itself in the poor, and the poor do not recognize Christ in the Church. But this situation is one of lost identity, or self-alienation for the Church, a situation in which the Church is not altogether the Church. The Church which is not the Church of the poor puts in serious jeopardy its churchly character. Therefore this becomes an ecclesiological criterion." [12]

That is to say, when the Church is open to the presence of Christ among the poor, to the meaning of his action in society and to his demands to satisfy their needs, it is also open to any other intervention by God in human life. Closing oneself to this fact is equivalent to ignoring the meaning of the Saviour's birth in the manger at Bethlehem, and the tremendous mystery of the Incarnation (Phil. 2 : 5-8).

To sum up, the importance of the poor in the message of Jesus can be seen fundamentally in the life of the Nazarene himself: Jesus' whole existence is a clear demonstration of what it was to be really poor. He was the full incarnation of the "servant of the Lord", through whom is fulfilled the justice of God (Isa. 53 : cf. Mark 14 : 50–16 : 8). Those who are poor in this world can have confidence in this life full of fruit, the seeds of deep hope, the expression of justice and love. The way in which Jesus drew near to the poor, taking them into account, sharing so many things with them, shows that God does not forget them. Although the life of the poor seems to be a sterile tree (like Hannah, the mother of Samuel, who for a long time had no children), they can continue to live in hope, for God has not left them to one side. Examples of such poor were Mary, the Lord's mother, and Simeon (Luke 2: 25-32); despite the setbacks and pain they each had to suffer, they could see the glory of God and — even more important — they could be instruments of his will. They were not people who sought material poverty because it represented some virtue, neither did they feel spiritually superior or great. Rather, they were poor people who were ready to share with others the little they had (and therefore ready to practise brotherly charity), not making their humble condition a motive for pride, but neither were they greedy for riches. In reality, their poverty was linked with a total and absolute trust in God, shown in a limitless availability to the Lord. Instead of keeping things for themselves, the truly poor are ready to share what they have with those who in any way live in humility. That is why the poor, although lacking in material possessions, try at least to share their hopes. The witness of the poor of Yahweh is seen in their active waiting for the Kingdom and its justice, and not by the cultivation of poverty as if it were an ideal for life.

NOTES:

[1] BÉDA RIGAUX: "Le Radicalisme du Règne" in *La Pauvreté Evangélique*, p. 151. Paris: Ed. du Cerf, 1971. The Qumran manuscripts give us an idea of the "rule of the community" whose members "separated themselves from the wicked and united themselves in doctrine and possessions" (l.Q.S. V, 2.9), quoted by JEAN COLSON in *Le Sacerdoce du Pauvre*, pp. 12-13. Paris: Ed. SOS, 1971.

[2] RUDOLF BULTMANN: *Primitive Christianity*, p. 76 ff. New York: Meridian Books (tr. R. H. Fuller), 1956.

[3] ERNST TROELTSCH: *The Social Teaching of the Christian Churches*, Vol. I, p. 51. London: George Allen & Unwin; New York: Macmillan Co., third impression, 1950. "Amidst all the uncertainties of tradition, the fundamental idea underlying the preaching of Jesus is easy to discern. It deals with the proclamation of the great final judgment, of the coming of the 'Kingdom of God', by which is meant that state of life in which God will have supreme control, when his will will be done on earth as it is now being done only in heaven; in this 'Kingdom', sin, suffering and pain will have been overcome, and the true spiritual values, combined with single-eyed devotion to the will of God, will shine out in the glory that is their due."

[4] J. DUPONT: "Les Pauvres et la Pauvreté dans les Evangiles et les Actes" in *La Pauvreté Evangélique*, *op. cit.*, pp. 50-51.

[5] A. GELIN: *Les Pauvres de Yahvé*, p. 145. Paris: Ed. du Cerf, 1953.

[6] Quoted by A. PÉRY in "Pauvre" in *Vocabulaire Biblique*, p. 222. Neuchâtel and Paris: Delachaux et Niestlé, second edition, 1956.

[7] J. DUPONT: *op. cit.*, pp. 48-49.

[8] GUSTAVO GUTIERREZ: *A Theology of Liberation*, p. 298 ff. Maryknoll, New York: Orbis Books, 1973.

[9] J. DUPONT: *op. cit.*, p. 52.

[10] A. PÉRY: *op. cit.*, p. 222.

[11] ST JOHN CHRYSOSTOMOS: *Sobre el Genesis*, MPG, T. LIV, col. 450.

[12] J. MÍGUEZ BONINO: "The Struggle of the Poor and the Church" in *The Ecumenical Review*, Vol. 28, No. 1, pp. 40-41. Geneva: World Council of Churches, January 1975.

3 · The Call to the Rich: To Follow Jesus

Since wealth and poverty are correlative terms, we must continue our study by analyzing the attitude and message of Jesus to the rich. We know that there were people of high social status who listened to his preaching, although they were not members of the closest group of the disciples. Several publicans opened their hearts to Jesus' demands (Matt. 9 : 9; Luke 5 : 27-32; Luke 19 : 1-10), and "a respected member of the council", Joseph of Arimathea, must have been close to his circle of followers, since St Mark's gospel says he "was also himself looking for the Kingdom of God", and it was he who asked for the body of Jesus. All this indicates that Jesus did not reject the rich, but rather that He challenged them in various ways to follow the path of justice and to be converted. However, his message was extremely hard for those who placed their hopes in wealth: the Lord referred to them as "fools" (Luke 12 : 16-21), since wealth can justify no man before God, especially when its possession is not accompanied by social responsibility (cf. the parable of the rich man and Lazarus: Luke 16 : 13-31). In the passage which precedes this story, Jesus clearly defines his position in relation to the problem of wealth: "No servant can serve two masters; for either he will hate the one and love the other, or he will be devoted to the one and despise the other. *You cannot serve God and Mammon*" (Luke 16 : 13), which finds a parallel in Matthew 6 : 24 in the Sermon on the Mount, which is followed by Jesus' recommendations to trust in providence and the loving care of God, first seeking "his Kingdom and his righteousness", and all other needs will be supplied (Matt. 6 : 25-34). Here, again, we find another description of the attitude of "the poor of Yahweh" who set their gaze on the fulfilment of the divine promises and do not base their existence on earthly treasures.

The radical nature of Jesus' message can be seen especially in his challenge to the rich; however respectable and gracious they were, Jesus always asked them in no uncertain terms to give up unconditionally their attachment to wealth. Jesus' position is clear: man cannot serve two masters. He who seeks to be his disciple cannot have two loyalties: "If any one comes to me and does not hate his own father and mother and wife and children and brothers and sisters, yes, and even his own life, he cannot be my disciple. Whoever does not bear his own cross and come after me, cannot be my disciple. For which of you, desiring to build a tower, does not first sit down and count the cost, whether he has enough to complete it? Otherwise, when he has laid a foundation, and is not able to finish, all who see it begin to mock him, saying, 'This man began to build, and was not able to finish.' Or what king, going to encounter another king in war, will not sit down first and take counsel whether he is able with ten thousand to meet him who comes against him with twenty thousand? And if not, while the other is yet a great way off, he sends an embassy and asks terms of peace. So therefore, whoever of you does not renounce all that he has cannot be my disciple" (Luke 14 : 26-33). The invitation to follow Jesus permits no comparisons or degrees; we must put aside not only wealth but even the emergencies of everyday life if we want to be faithful to that call (Luke 9 : 57-62).

A clear example of this is the story of the "rich young man" who approached Jesus, wanting to be his disciple. The gospel text is eloquent, and relevant to the question we are considering in this chapter: "And as He (Jesus) was setting out on his journey, a man ran up and knelt before him, and asked him, 'Good Teacher, what must I do to inherit eternal life?' And Jesus said to him, 'Why do you call me good? No one is good but God alone. You know the commandments: 'Do not kill, Do not commit adultery, Do not steal, Do not bear false witness, Do not defraud, Honour your father and your mother.' And he said to him, 'Teacher, all these I have observed from my youth.' And Jesus looking upon him loved him, and said to him, 'You lack one thing; go, sell what you have and give to the poor, and you will have treasure in heaven; and come, follow me.' At that saying his countenance fell, and he went away sorrowful; for he had great possessions. And Jesus looked around and said to his disciples, 'How hard it will be for those who have riches to enter the Kingdom of God!' And the disciples were amazed at his words. But Jesus said to them again, 'Children, how hard it is to enter the

Kingdom of God! It is easier for a camel to go through the eye of a needle than for a rich man to enter the Kingdom of God.' " (Mark 10 : 17-25: cf. also Matt. 19 : 16-30; Luke 18 : 18-30). What are the implications of this call?

The duty of "almsgiving"

Jesus said to the rich man: "Sell what you have, and give to the poor." The Greek term used is *ptôchos*, which includes all kinds of poor: the weak, the deprived, the helpless and needy, and so on. They are the ones who, at a time when the coming of the Kingdom was expected, deserved a sign of justice which already announced the day when, through the saving action of God, his will should be done "on earth as it is in heaven". For the rich man, this demand that he share his wealth with the poor would be evidence of his anxious anticipation of the Kingdom of righteousness. To put this in another way: "The rejection of earthly goods is part of this eschatology. The end is not only a motive. That end creates a spiritual state and permits a just appreciation of the new values." [1] More than this, this rejection of the wealth of this world in favour of those who have none is a clear sign and evidence that a fundamental change has taken place in the rich man's heart: instead of concentrating greedily on himself, he now practises brotherly charity, especially responsibility to the underprivileged. This transformation is conversion, the passage from the old man to the new creation, who takes his place in history in an attitude of total dependence on the Kingdom which is to come and to the person of Jesus, the Master who proclaims it.

The call of Jesus goes to the very root of things, but it in no sense implies a rejection of what life can offer. Ernst Troeltsch saw this very clearly when he said: "Christ requires men to be indifferent to material happiness and to money, to practise sexual self-restraint, to have a mind that values the unseen and eternal more than the seen and temporal, and finally to develop a personality which in its central aim is thoroughly harmonious and unified. Here the Gospel is extremely radical. It is not ascetic, but it is very severe; no doubt about the possibility of its practical realization if permitted; yet this austerity in no way destroys the innocent joy of life." [2] In other words, none of these requirements indicate values which are justifiable in themselves. They point to the fact that following the path shown us by the Master requires absolute acceptance of his will. The disciple cannot be incoherent nor ambivalent. "The radicalism of the teachings of Jesus on the goods of this world and the poor cannot be separated from the radicalism which characterizes the relationship between Master and disciple." [3] The demand to the rich man to give "alms" is placed within the framework of Christian discipleship. Here we must recognize that the use of language can confuse our interpretation. In current usage, the term refers to a gift offered to the needy for love of God. This gift very often has no profound effect on the life of the receiver, and it is generally understood as assistance which alleviates his condition without allowing him to overcome it. The term comes from the Latin *alimosna*, from the Greek *elemosyne*, used by the LXX translators to indicate *an action of justice* (the Sedaqa) which, according to the Old Testament, is in accordance with the fulfilment of the will of God. Consequently, the duty of almsgiving should not be understood as the gift of something which causes us great problems if we are deprived of it, *but rather as a sign* of the saving justice of the Kingdom.

The radical nature of the duty is clear, and it denotes the high price to be paid if we seek to be disciples of Jesus.

"Called to follow Jesus in his itinerant ministry, the disciples had to abandon their goods (Mark 1 : 18-20; Matt. 9 : 20-22; Luke 18 : 28, and others), *all* that they had (Luke 5 : 11; 28; Mark 10 : 28; Matt. 19 : 27). The rich man who seeks to follow Jesus is faced with the same requirement (Mark 10 : 21; Matt. 19 : 21; Luke 18 : 22). This demand permits the elimination of candidates who hope to follow Jesus but are insufficiently prepared (Matt. 8 : 18-22; Luke 9 : 57-62). How can they follow the 'Son of Man' who has nowhere to lay his head? (Matt. 8 : 20; Luke 9 : 58). In response to Peter's comment: 'Lo, we have left everything and followed you', Jesus replies with a promise which widens the horizon: it is addressed to everyone who, for his sake, has abandoned his home, brothers, sisters, mother, father, children or possessions (Mark 10 : 28-29). The two parables of the man who builds a tower and the king who goes to war end in St Luke's gospel with a general declaration: 'So therefore, whoever of you does not renounce all that he has cannot be my disciple' (Luke 14 : 33). In other passages, we find the affirmation of the need to take up our cross if we seek to follow Jesus (Mark 8 : 34; Matt. 16 : 24; Luke 9 : 33), and in other passages it is linked with an even more absolute demand: 'Whoever would save his life will lose it, and whoever loses his life for my sake will find it' (Matt.

16 : 25; Mark 8 : 35; Luke 9 : 24; cf. also Matt. 10 : 39; Luke 17 : 33; John 12 : 25)." [4]

The disciple shows his unconditional readiness to follow his master by selling all he has to give to the poor. Material possessions tie people down in various ways. He who follows the Son of Man must be ready to make the sacrifices required of him, as a sign of the kind of justice which he hopes for with the coming of the Kingdom of God. Those who possess wealth are called to practise this kind of witness.

On the other hand, the completion of Jesus' mission to his disciples requires a total self-denial, but at the same time great foresight. This can be seen in the mandate given by Jesus to the twelve and to the seventy (Mark 6 : 8-9; Matt. 10 : 9-10; Luke 9 : 3): they must take nothing with them while they are on mission except what is strictly necessary: neither bag, nor money, nor a spare tunic, not even food. However, at the Last Supper, according to St Luke's version, when He was telling the disciples about the difficulties of the times to come, Jesus says that he who has a purse should take it with him, as well as a bag and even a sword (Luke 22 : 36). Although the terms may appear contradictory, the requirement is the same. During the period of the ministry of Jesus, a happy time, the apostolate was bearable despite the difficult demands: those who were open to the message of the Master shared what they had with the emissaries of the Nazarene. But from the moment of Jesus' passion, the radical nature of the requirements placed on the disciples meant they must be ready to face hitherto unsuspected difficulties and meet them with the necessary means (which of course were not *all* the means, but those required by the nature of the mission which had been entrusted to them). From that time, they should expect hostility from those who rejected the message of Jesus. If they were attacked, the disciples would have to defend themselves (as is suggested here by the image of the sword, although we do not believe it was to be taken literally). [5]

We believe, then, that the interpretation that the renunciation of material goods is to be seen in the context of the call *to follow Jesus (sequela Christi)* is confirmed. According to the various gospel passages we have quoted, the unconditional nature of the demand touches three aspects of human existence which determine the slant they aim to give it. As we have seen, the nature of discipleship demands, first of all, leaving one's family for the love of the

Master. Second, the carrying of one's cross in the steps of Jesus (that is, to deny oneself, even as far as attaching little importance to life itself). Thirdly, renouncing all material possessions in favour of the poor. This last aspect indicates once again that poverty is considered to be neither a virtue nor an ideal. To practise "alms-giving" by assuming poverty is to show that one is ready to participate in the life of the community of those who hope only in the manifestation of the love and justice of God.

However, in the writings of the New Testament, and particularly the Epistle of the Apostle Paul to the Philippians, we find a signpost which can help us on our way. In the famous text of chapter 2, verses 5-11, in which the author describes the process followed by God in Christ so that "every tongue (may) confess that Jesus Christ is Lord", there is a suggestion that the *"sequela Christi"* presumes a sharing in the mystery of the humility of Christ, who not only denied himself by assuming human existence, but also adopted in it the role of a servant, obedient even unto death on the cross. This suggestion, taken to its ultimate implications, brings the believer to communion with the Lord Jesus Christ, who "for your sake became poor, so that by his poverty you might become rich" (II Cor. 8 : 9). This signpost offered by the Pauline interpretation clearly corresponds to a post-pascal reading of the life, death and resurrection of Jesus. It insists, and in this sense also corroborates, that the self-denial, the impoverishment, of those who believe in Jesus must never be taken as a requirement in itself which acquires the character of a law, but rather something which is to be expected when we live as followers of Jesus, something which leads to the acceptance of total openness to Jesus and the renunciation of anything which can separate us from the fulfilment of his will which aims always at the establishment of his justice. And this supposes the practice of brotherly love towards the poor. Hence the need to carry out the duty of "almsgiving", not because it is a rule in itself, but because "the love of Christ controls us" (II Cor. 5 : 14).[6] St Basil, in his *Great Rules*, says that being a disciple means renouncing the things of the world, sharing what we have with the poor, "because only thus can we live according to the Gospel".[7]

God or Mammon

According to the Synoptic Gospels, the alternative is clear: God or wealth. We have already emphasized that the radical nature of the call of Jesus cannot be compared with any other requirement. The Master says that wealth is an obstacle to discipleship and the expectation of the Kingdom of God; those who are disciples must share their wealth with others, as a means of witnessing to his justice. Thus the Scriptures do not look upon wealth with approval. In the Old Testament, and especially in the book of Job, there are already references to the transitory nature of any kind of material possession (cf. Job 24 : 24; 27 : 13-23, and also I Sam. 2 : 5-7; Ps. 49 : 16-20, and others). However, there are passages which indicate that the satisfaction of material needs is also considered as a blessing from God, especially in the extracanonic literature (cf. Ecclus. 11 : 17-22). In any case, wealth is *always* considered as something which does not help the human being to receive the justice of God. Thus, for example, the Wisdom literature states that the fear of God is more important than striving for the goods of this world (Prov. 15 : 16; 16 : 8). This is still further emphasized by some of the Psalms, in passages such as Psalm 37 : 15-16: "Better is a little that the righteous has than the abundance of many wicked. For the arms of the wicked shall be broken; but the Lord upholds the righteous." [8] It would be incorrect, though, to say that the alternative proposed by Jesus can already be seen in the Old Testament. However, the passion of some of the prophets, who even risked their lives (Jeremiah, for example), is in a way a prelude to what Jesus so clearly proposes some centuries later. In other words, while the Old Testament points to the transitory nature of material possessions, there is no explicit invitation to renounce the accumulation of fortune. This is precisely the news which Jesus brings.

It was Jesus who pointed clearly to the demonic power of money, calling it *Mammon* (Matt. 6 : 24; Luke 16 : 13). Jacques Ellul, in a study carried out more than twenty years ago but which is still a classic on the subject, says : "As we know, this is an Aramaic word which in general means money, but which can also refer to wealth. Here Jesus bestows a personality on money and considers it as a form of divinity. Now, this does not have its origin in the surroundings. Jesus did not take this word from common usage in the circles to which he addressed it, since no divinity of that name appears to have been known either in Jewish or Gallilean circles, nor among the nearby pagan groups. Jesus is not using the name of a pagan divinity to make people understand that it is a question of choosing between the true God and a false god. Neither does it refer to a superstition current in society which would be more or less common to all. This personification of money seems to be a creation of Jesus himself, and if this is true, it shows us something exceptional about money, since Jesus was not in the habit of making such personifications or comparisons with divinity." [9]

It is as if Jesus saw in money a power which could oppose God. That power is what leads to the deterioration of human relationships, because "they sell the righteous for silver and the needy for a pair of shoes" (Amos 2 : 6). In this sense, before the authority of the Master, money plays the part of a counterpower which has taken different forms throughout history to denaturalize the creation of God and place obstacles to the fulfilment of his will. Money, of course, also symbolizes human interests which dominate and enslave, conquer and rule, control and censure. As a symbol, it denotes a power which contradicts the authority of Jesus. It is what led Ananias and Sapphira to break the implicit rules of the fraternal community of Jerusalem. It was also for "thirty pieces of silver" that Judas betrayed Jesus (Matt. 26 : 15). The soldiers who were astonished by the miracle of the resurrection received "much money" not to tell the truth about what had happened. There can therefore be no compromise between the God of justice and the power generated by injustice and exploitation; for this same reason we are to render unto Caesar what is Caesar's (money) but to God we owe our whole-hearted love and obedience (Matt. 22 : 21).

This perspective on the meaning of money is underlined by the first Epistle to Timothy, 6 : 10 : "the love of money is the root of all evil", a declaration which is first found in the Old Testament in the book of Ecclesiastes, 5 : 10: "He who loves money will not be satisfied with money; nor he who loves wealth, with gain: this also is vanity." In other words, wealth implies continual servitude. It was not for nothing that the Mosaic legislation was concerned to reduce and limit the possibilities of money, forbidding usury and lending for interest (Deut. 23 : 20; Lev. 25 : 35-36; Ex. 22 : 25 ff.).

The eschatological expectation which is always present in the message of Jesus could not accept that the abundance of goods possessed should close anyone's heart to the justice of the Kingdom of God and his requirement of brotherly love. He who submits to the power of money is not fit for the Kingdom which is to come. This is why it is difficult for the rich to enter into the Kingdom of heaven.

"How dangerous it is to be rich! Most men are tied to possessions and earthly worries; they are delighted to be invited to share in the salvation prepared by God, but when they have to make their choice, they escape from the decision like the guests who had accepted an invitation to dinner, but when the time came they excused themselves, saying they had no time (Luke 14 : 15-21; Matt. 22 : 1–10). We must be ready to sacrifice everything for the Kingdom of God, like a man who finds a treasure in a field and goes and sells everything he owns to be able to buy it, or the merchant who sells everything he has so as to possess a pearl of great worth (Matt. 13 : 44-46). 'If your right eye causes you to sin, pluck it out and throw it away; it is better that you lose one of your members than that your whole body be thrown into hell' (Matt. 5 : 29). This renunciation of the goods of this world is not an escape from the world, a form of asceticism, but rather a separation from the world which reflects an attitude of readiness to obey the demands of God who encourages us to free ourselves from all the bonds which tie us to the world. This renunciation is linked positively with the commandment of love, through which man turns away from himself so as to be ready to meet his neighbour. In choosing his neighbour, he has made a choice for God." [10]

The basic purpose of the Gospel, then, justifies a rigorous attitude towards the rich and those who are bound by wealth. In St Luke's gospel, therefore, the blessing of the poor is almost immediately followed by a series of very strong words to those whose existence is in any way assured in worldly terms: "But woe to you that are rich, for you have received your consolation. Woe to you that are full now, for you shall hunger. Woe to you that laugh now, for you shall mourn and weep. Woe to you, when all men speak well of you, for so their father did to the false prophets" (Luke 6 : 24-26). This hardness is even more visible in the parable of the rich man and poor Lazarus (Luke 16 : 19-31), and it was maintained through the early years of Christian history until it was reflected in the words of the Epistle of James (to which we will return in the following chapter). Wealth prevents the rich from accepting the authority of the Master, and for this very reason "they much prefer to serve human laws, which allow the greatest and most powerful — that is the rich — to place themselves above others and make their power felt over them" (Mark 10 : 42).[11]

The text from James explains why the choice between God and wealth is unavoidable: he who serves riches is an instrument of injustice in the world, his sin is to abuse the poor: "Come now, you rich, weep and howl for the miseries that are coming upon you. Your riches have rotted and your garments are motheaten. Your gold and silver have rusted, and their rust will be evidence against you and will eat your flesh like fire. You have laid up treasure for the last days. Behold, the wages of the labourers who mow your fields, which you kept back by fraud, cry out; and the cries of the harvesters have reached the ears of the Lord of hosts. You have lived on this earth in luxury and in pleasure; you have fattened your hearts in a day of slaughter. You have condemned, you have killed the righteous man; he does not resist you" (James 5 : 1-6). The last sentence of this passage is an allusion to the fundamental contradiction experienced by the rich in face of someone who, like Jesus, is just *par excellence*. The challenge Jesus presents to the rich must be resolved in the heart of man. Jesus tries to convince, while the rich, faithful to the logic of the power of money, win by conquest. In practice, Jesus did not rebel against his sentence nor his suffering. But his radical requirement to choose between God or Mammon cannot be ignored.

The rich man hopes to save himself by the accumulation of capital. Jesus, on the other hand, proclaims the need to give oneself up to divine providence. The temptation of the rich man, into which he constantly falls unless he changes radically, is to seek total security in his fortune. Jesus describes this as a terrible illusion: "Take heed, and beware of all covetousness; for a man's life does not consist in the abundance of his possessions" (Luke 12 : 15, and especially the verses which follow with the parable of the foolish rich man). Instead of attaching importance to material things because of the feeling of security which they seem to give, Jesus wants his disciples to place their trust in God alone. Consequently, if the attraction of possessions can jeopardize the salvation of those who seek to accumulate them, they must not hesitate to get rid of them all, lest by wanting to possess everything, they lose it all. This seems to be the meaning of the choice which Jesus presents. The danger of riches is so great that we should not be careless and run any kind of risk for them. Jesus does not present this separation from material goods only negatively: he also presents an attitude which is radically opposed to the greed for wealth — total trust in God. This does not mean that Jesus ignores the fact that man's material needs must be resolved. Not in vain did he say that man does not live by bread alone, which also supposes that he cannot live without bread. This is why the prayer he taught to his disciples says: "Give us this day our daily bread." But to ask for bread for today does not mean wanting bread for always, even beyond death, nor more bread than is necessary, especially when the accumulation of this wealth often implies that others go without their daily bread.

The road we must follow

To go back to what we have already suggested, we believe there is a danger in the simplification which suggests that following Christ consists in being poor. Rather, as is implicit in the call to the disciples, the path indicated by Jesus is not poverty in itself, but the life of love, which must necessarily take the form of charity towards the needy — solidarity with the poor and exploited. This is why the Christians of the communities in the first century of the Church's history were ready to share. The road proposed to us is not that of poverty, but that of charity, implicit in the duty of "almsgiving".

It was Christ himself who sketched out for us the impoverishment which we are called to assume. According to the text already quoted from II Corinthians 8 : 9, He who was rich became poor so that we could become rich. This style of living becomes clear on Calvary. The cross shows that the disciple is called to participate in the painful and constant effort of God, until his reign finally comes, to reinstate the ways of justice which men have distorted and destroyed through love of wealth and greed for power. This means we must become incarnate (as God was incarnate in Jesus Christ), identifying ourselves with the victims of injustice, who hope for a better tomorrow. For these, there is no glory, but the persistent reality of the cross. In other words, those who claim to be disciples of Jesus cannot participate in the social processes of our time with the perspective of triumphalism, but with the openness of the Suffering Servant, the true "poor of Yahweh". As Gustavo Gutierrez says, Jesus does not assume the condition of poverty and its tremendous consequences with the purpose of idealizing it, but "because of love for and solidarity with men who suffer in it. It is to redeem them from their sin and to enrich them with his poverty. It is to struggle against human selfishness and everything that divides men and causes there to be rich and poor, possessors and dispossessed, oppressors and oppressed.

"Poverty is an act of love and liberation. It has a redemptive value. If the ultimate cause of man's exploitation and alienation is selfishness, the deepest reason for voluntary poverty is love of neighbour. Christian poverty has meaning only as a commitment of solidarity with the poor, with those who suffer misery and injustice. The commitment is to witness to the evil which has resulted from sin and is a breach of communion. It is not a question of idealizing poverty, but rather of taking it on as it is — an evil — to protest against it and to struggle to abolish it. As Ricoeur says, you cannot really be with the poor unless you are struggling against poverty. Because of this solidarity — which must manifest itself in specific action, a style of life, a break with one's social class — one can also help the poor and exploited to become aware of their exploitation and seek liberation from it. Christian poverty, an expression of love, is solidarity *with the poor* and is a protest *against poverty*. This is the concrete, contemporary meaning of the witness of poverty. It is a poverty lived not for its own sake, but rather as an authentic imitation of Christ; it is a poverty which means taking on the sinful condition of man to liberate him from sin and all its consequences." [12]

To conclude this chapter, we should add that the *sequela Christi*, when it is taken on with all its implications, leads to an *imitatio Christi* — to the inevitability of the cross. The challenge of the poor and poverty to the community of faith should provoke an attitude of witness, of militance, of a prophetic nature in this community: an announcement of the justice of God and a denouncement of the injustice of men. It is not something which can be defined in words alone, but a way of living. The rejection of riches, and brotherly love for one's neighbour in need is the sign of total acceptance of Jesus and openness to the Kingdom which is to come.

NOTES:

[1] BÉDA RIGAUX: "Le Radicalisme du Règne" in *La Pauvreté Evangélique*, p. 171. Paris: Ed. du Cerf, 1971.

[2] ERNST TROELTSCH: *The Social Teaching of the Christian Churches*, Vol. I, p. 54. London: George Allen & Unwin; New York: Macmillan Co. third impression, 1950.

[3] BÉDA RIGAUX: *op. cit.*, pp. 137-138.

[4] J. DUPONT: "Les Pauvres et la Pauvreté dans les Evangiles et les Actes" in *La Pauvreté Evangélique, op. cit.*, pp. 53-55.

[5] Cf. J. DUPONT: *op. cit.*, p. 57.

[6] Cf. F. BERTRAM CLOGG: *The Christian Character in the Early Church*, pp. 92-93. London: Epworth Press, 1944. Subsequent to the *sequela Christi*, the disciples are called to "deny themselves", "to take up their cross", to "live for others", and to "grow according to the stature of Christ".

[7] St BASIL: *Great Rules*, MPG, T. XXXI, Col. 919-934.

[8] Cf. for example, *Psalms* 73 : 25-28; 84 : 11, etc.

[9] JACQUES ELLUL: "L'Argent", in *Etudes Théologiques et Religieuses*, 27th year, No. 4, p. 31.

[10] RUDOLF BULTMANN: *Le Christianisme Primitif*, pp. 104-105. Paris: Payot, 1969.

[11] HELGA RUSCHE: *L'Epître de St Jacques*, pp. 38-39. Le Pury & Lyon: Ed. Xavier Maffrus, 1967.

[12] GUSTAVO GUTIERREZ: *A Theology of Liberation*, pp. 300-301. London: SCM Press, 1974.

4 · The Poor and Poverty in the Church of the First Century

What has been discussed in the two preceding chapters could also come under this heading. Indeed, if we remember that the gospel stories not only reproduce the oral tradition of the early Church concerning the sayings and life of Jesus, but also reflect the interpretations given to them by the various Christian communities within which the gospels were written, we must conclude that the emphases of these texts offer some indications as to how the different congregations of the time saw the challenge of the poor and poverty. Today, it is generally accepted that the author of St Mark's gospel based his writing on a source ("Q") derived from a collection of the sayings of Jesus, as recalled by those nearest the Master — people who were certainly members of the Christian community in Jerusalem, which was marked by a strong eschatological influence. However, St Matthew's gospel seems to have taken shape in the context of the communities which grew up through the Church's missionary work in Syria where the Judaism of the scribes predominated, which must have been reflected one way or another in this text.[1] St Luke's gospel and the book of Acts reflect the interpretation of the communities influenced by the missionary work of the Apostle Paul, although it is important to note that their author shows an interest in social questions which is less obvious in the thinking of St Paul, at least as it appears in the Pauline texts available today (the epistles of the "*corpus paulino*").

Our analysis so far is not enough to give us an adequate understanding of the matter, and we must examine other texts as well. But first, we must consider the context in which they were written. In those days, when Rome's domination had spread throughout the Mediterranean, constituting the most extensive empire the region had ever known, the definition of rich and poor was based on the ownership of property, and especially buildings. Those who had them were powerful; ownership was seen as the foundation of happiness, giving the right to freedom and independence, and a sign of power. The lack of property was synonymous with dependence and with the obligation to earn one's daily bread by work which was considered to be inferior. Slaves, of course, were held to be even lower than the "poor". So "poverty" and "wealth" were opposite terms. In the Roman world of the generations which followed immediately after the death of Jesus Christ, poverty indicated the lack — even privation — of goods which guaranteed the realization of full human potential; the lack of property placed enormous limits on the satisfaction of vital needs, and indicated insufficient social and political influence, besides the absence of any obvious economic security. "Poverty was a negative term, while wealth was considered positive." [2]

It was inevitable, then, in view of the message of Jesus which we have already discussed, that the Church should attract the humble and disinherited who constituted the great mass of the peoples on whom Rome imposed its rule. Sergio Rostagno, applying a materialist understanding of the New Testament, suggests that the words of Jesus related by the Apostle Paul, among others, must necessarily have awoken expectations and hopes of a "revolutionary" kind, encouraging the attraction of the humblest sectors of society towards the Church. This seems to be the explanation of I Corinthians 1 : 26-31: "For consider your call, brethren; not many of you were wise according to worldly standards, not many powerful, not many were of noble birth; but God chose what is foolish in the world to shame the wise, God chose what is weak in the world to shame the strong, God chose what is low and despised in the world, even things that are not, to bring to nothing things that are, so that no human being might boast in the presence of God. He is the source of your life in Christ Jesus, whom God made our wisdom, our righteousness and sanctification and redemption; therefore, as it is written, 'Let him who boasts, boast of the Lord.'" The Lord's acceptance of the Gentiles and pagans which constitutes one of the basic elements of St Paul's preaching must be understood as the confirmation in history of the fulfilment of God's justice with the coming of the Kingdom of God. "It is not irrelevant that as well as working through the extraordinary (and paradoxical) event of the conversion of the Gentiles, the Gospel should also work through a form of social revolution.

The one is as Pauline as the other, and this is what I wanted to bring out. God chooses the weak classes to overthrow the unjust and oppressive structure of the world: that thesis is biblical, it is Pauline and it belongs at the centre of the Apostle's theology." [3] This quotation supports the position that the attraction of the new Christian communities for the poor did not encourage them to escape from the world and ignore their social condition, but to assume it fully.

This attraction, by the way, was not exclusive to the first century A.D.; a couple of centuries later, it became more marked. Many of the names clumsily carved on the walls of the Roman catacombs were certainly those of slaves who were freed, but never became rich — Stefanas, Fortunatus, Acaicus, Amplias, Urbanus, Herodion, Hermas, and so on.[4] Their awareness of their social condition, in the ideological and political framework of that time, strengthened their hope in the coming of the Kingdom of God and the imminent return of the Lord, whom they awaited so anxiously. This hope, in turn, inspired the Church's missionary work, whose rapid expansion was due to the affinity between the aspirations of these sectors of society and the content of the Gospel message which was presented to them. Thus Ernst Troeltsch says: "Further, the message of Jesus also deals with the formation of the community based on the hope of the Kingdom which, in the meantime, possesses both the pledge of the Kingdom and the preparation for its coming in Jesus himself. The community is to be founded by the missionary efforts of the narrower circles of the immediate disciples and followers of Jesus; they therefore are entrusted with the special duties which devolve upon the heralds of the Kingdom. With their help, the Kingdom is preached everywhere." [5]

However, in spite of this undeniable interest which the Gospel aroused among the poorest people of the time, thinking and practice on the problem of poverty in the various Christian communities was not homogeneous. At times, the texts even seem to reveal serious contradictions. We shall try to clarify this by considering three different experiences: the primitive community of Jerusalem, according to the testimony of the book of Acts; the writings of Paul on this subject, which must to some degree reflect the practice of the various Pauline communities which responded to the challenge of the poor, and lastly the message of the Epistle of James whose radical position on this matter is well known.

The primitive Christian community in Jerusalem

There is no evidence that the community in Jerusalem included people with power or strong social influence. The book of Acts says they were ordinary people with varying amounts of possessions, but who were ready to share them. The atmosphere of prayer and expectation of the imminent coming of the Holy Spirit and the return of the Lord indicates that their members came from the category that we can describe as "the poor of Yahweh".

"The believers in Jesus belonged to those quiet, religious people who gladly gave themselves the name of 'the poor' as found in the Psalms, and who treasured with faithful hearts the sayings of the Master about the blessedness of the poor. At the same time, however, they knew themselves to be the saints, the faithful who were beloved by God, the remnant of the people separated off for the Last Day of which the prophets and the apocalyptists had spoken. Both names meant the same thing and described those whose hope and expectation was that the existing sad condition of the lowly and needy would soon end, and that they would be rewarded with overwhelming glory. The eschatological expectation of this original church, composed of Jews, is reflected in the shining allegories of the Revelation of John." [6]

The decisive experience in the formation of this community was the pouring out of the Holy Spirit in the days of Pentecost following the resurrection of Jesus Christ (Acts 2), which inspired the famous sermon of St Peter recorded there. Many were baptized as a consequence of this: "And they devoted themselves to the apostles' teaching and fellowship, to the breaking of bread, and prayers. And fear came upon every soul; and many wonders and signs were done through the apostles. And all who believed were together *and had all things in common; and sold their possessions and goods and distributed them to all, as any had need. And day by day, attending the temple together and breaking bread in their homes, they partook of food with glad and generous hearts*" (Acts 2 : 42-46, our emphasis).

One of the basic characteristics of the new community, then, was the common ownership of goods. Here, we might usefully quote J. Dupont, an authority on the matter: "The documents on the community of goods practised by the emerging Church in Jerusalem have reached us basically in two 'summaries', or recapitulative descriptions, in which the author seeks to give an overall view of the life of the first Christian group. We will limit our comments to what they contain. After relating the events of Pentecost and the many conversions which took place that day (Acts 2 : 1-41), Luke offers a first summary (Acts 2 : 42-47). Here, he deals mainly with the community life of those who were converted on the day of Pentecost. However, two verses have clearly been added later (44-45) about the community of goods, possibly provoked by the mention of *koinonía*, in which, according to verse 42, the believers persevered, an addition which anticipates the theme of the second summary, from which it has apparently been taken. The summary of chapter 4 (verses 32-35) refers properly to the community of goods, the expression of unanimity which reigned among the Christians. Here, again, there is an element of heterogeneity in verse 33, which speaks of a miraculous power exercised by the apostles, thus anticipating the theme of the third summary in 5 : 12-16. The basic text is composed of verses 32 and 34-35 of chapter 4, of which verses 44-45 of chapter 2 are an anticipatory echo." [7]

Here, we must ask: What is the significance of the community of goods in a group such as the primitive Christian church in Jerusalem? Basically, it reflects at the material level the kind of spiritual communion which should prevail in the Church. In other words, it is an expression of a deep fellowship, emphasized by the summary of chapter 4 : 32: "Now the company of those who believed were of one heart and soul." Since they share one faith, the unity of Christians is expressed above all in the union of the spirits of those who comprise the community; this is why they pray together, share the Eucharist in each other's homes, and meet together in the temple. This essential unanimity must be expressed at the material level as a sign of brotherly community. "The readiness to share goods is a consequence of their awareness that together they form one community, a body in which each feels solidarity with all the others." [8] Inevitably, this had the effect, particularly in the early days, of eliminating the poverty of many who joined the community. This can be seen in Acts 4 : 34: "There was not a needy person among them", which seems to confirm the promise found in Deuteronomy 15 : 4: "But there will be no poor among you." For the first Christians in Jerusalem, the existence of their community was the fulfilment of these words.

And here, we return to a point made several times in preceding chapters: goods are shared not to make oneself poor because poverty is seen as an ideal, but to vanquish and eradicate poverty, so that there shall be no more poor. The road we are shown, the ideal we are to pursue, is brotherly love, which is to be expressed by the act of sharing ("the duty of almsgiving") with the poor. Each is to receive "as any had need" (Acts 2 : 45; 4 : 35). Since it was to be a church in which no one lived in poverty and misfortune, J. Dupont rightly asks whether this could truly be called a "church of the poor"...[9]

According to R. Minnerath, the important point here is that it is impossible to consider a group as part of the people who witness to the Lord's resurrection (Acts 4 : 33) unless they practise the common administration of goods.[10] In other words, believing in the resurrection, living in the freedom of the Spirit, leaving aside the law and death, led to rejection of wealth and the yoke it imposes on people. This rejection (a negative act) has its positive complement in the practice of brotherly charity, as St John Chrysostomos rightly points out in his commentary on Acts 4 : 32-35: "Charity makes you see another self in your neighbour, and teaches you to rejoice in his goods as in your own, to tolerate his defects as your own. Charity makes one body of all, and of their souls, in which the Holy Spirit dwells. And thus the Spirit of peace does not rest on the separated, but on those whose souls are united. Charity makes what each owns the property of all, as is shown in the book of Acts." [11]

Now, this does not mean that the community of goods had the force of a law in the Jerusalem church; this would be a denial of the Gospel and the freedom which it brings. A quick reading of the story of Ananias and Sapphira (Acts 5 : 1-11), who sold a possession and did not give the whole of the proceeds to the community, might indicate that sharing goods was an obligation. The problem in this case lies not in the fact that they did not give the whole of the proceeds of the sale, but in their "contriving to defraud" the other members of the community by lying to them about the proceeds. It seems rather that each gave "according to his ability" (Acts 11 : 29) as is said concerning the relief sent by the brothers of the Antioch church to those who lived in Judea. So the practice of the community of goods did not imply the abolition of all types of private ownership, but demanded great honesty in the act of sharing, and it was a clear indication that they should not accumulate wealth, although small properties could be maintained, as the mother of John Mark did, recorded in Acts 12 : 12; she had not sold her house, and it was there that the brothers of Jerusalem met to pray. "The tradition which holds that individual ownership had been abolished in the church of

Jerusalem does not correspond to the truth. It is the result of generalization and the transposition of an exact event, such as the fact
that the Galilean colony lived in community and had, without doubt,
a common purse as was the case with the group formed by Jesus
and his disciples during his public ministry." [12]

The account of the ministry of the deacons (cf. Acts 6 : 1-6) shows
how the practice of brotherly charity and service was organized
following its early spontaneous manifestations. Notwithstanding the
importance of this, the story contains revealing signs of how demo-
cratically the Christian community in Jerusalem was organized.
Faced with the need to structure the services, the apostles did not
decide on their own authority who should carry out this ministry,
but brought it to the community of believers for discussion. This
indicates the predominance of a popular concept which, in the course
of history, has been characteristic of the most humble social sectors,
which have wherever possible proved resistant to accepting and
exercising authoritarian procedures for decision-making.[13]

The deep spiritual communion which can be seen on the one
hand in the community of goods and on the other in the sharing of
power, has been defined by Ernst Troeltsch as the consequence of the
revolutionary nature of Jesus' teaching on what the German historian
and sociologist has called "the communism of love".

"One of the permanent results of the teaching of Jesus, however,
was this idea of communism of love. In later ages, during times of
special need, there arose again and again the tendency to repeat the
same, or at least similar, experiments within the Church in other
forms. The theoretical expositions of the later Fathers of the Church
proclaim it in many ways as the genuine fundamental doctrine of
Christianity: free and common to all like light, air and earth, like
the fact that we are all come from God and to him we all return —
earthly possessions should be for the use of all through the love
which shares and keeps nothing back. When, at a later date, men
again tried to construct a purely abstract theory out of Jesus' exhortations on social questions — that is, when men tried to reduce the
absolute readiness of love to sacrifice, into a theory — this always led
quite logically to a fresh attempt to realize the communism of love.
The monastic system, the medieval communistic movements, the
Anabaptists, modern fanatics and idealists have all followed this
clue. This idea contains a revolutionary element, although it has
no desire for revolution." [14]

St Paul on poverty and assistance to the poor

We have already mentioned some of the indications offered in the thinking of St Paul concerning the attitude of the Christian community towards the challenge of the poor, namely, the importance of taking into account the road taken by God in Jesus Christ so that men could accept the will of the Lord and recognize it as such. We have also mentioned the comments of Sergio Rostagno, applying a "materialistic" interpretation to I Corinthians. However, in St Paul, we see a different practice and understanding of the problem. His position is well known; on more than one occasion it led to vigorous arguments with the leaders of the Jerusalem community, particularly Peter. Paul insisted on the need to preach the Gospel to the Gentiles, without imposing upon them the demands of the law, and this brought severe criticism from those whose concept of Christianity was closely linked with the existence and perspectives of the Jewish people. The controversy began to take a more structured form, and certain points of compromise were reached on the occasion of the council (synod?) of Jerusalem (43-44 A.D.) recorded in chapter 15 of the book of Acts. Among other things, the compromise gave Paul the possibility of going out on mission to the Gentiles on condition that he should "remember the poor" (Gal. 2 : 10). What could have been the meaning of this condition? [15] For some, it is a confirmation of the mandate of Jesus, but to others (including Goguel), it is a way of recognizing the special importance of the Jerusalem community among the first century churches, which seems to be corroborated by Paul's words in his Epistle to the Romans (cf. 15 : 25-27) concerning the collection organized in favour of "the saints" of Jerusalem among the churches of the Gentile world.

To the apostle to the Gentiles, the collection for the first Christian community offers an opportunity to expound his own concept of money and of justice. Thus he writes to the Corinthians: "I do not mean that others should be eased and you burdened, but that as a matter of *equality* your abundance at the present time should supply their want, so that their abundance may supply your want, that there may be equality" (II Cor. 8 : 13-14). On the one hand, St Paul believes that money can also serve good causes, in particular that of brotherly love between the faithful. On the other hand, the interchange between material and spiritual gifts can help to reestablish a certain degree of equality among people. This supposes, though it is not explicitly stated by the apostle, that money (which is so severely judged by Jesus because of what it represents) can be redeemed. In fact, money can also symbolize the bond that unites those who form one community of brothers in different places. Thus, after writing to Timothy that "the love of money is the root of all evil" (I Tim. 6 : 10), he adds to his advice to the rich: "They are to do good, to be rich in good deeds, liberal and generous, thus laying up for themselves a good foundation for the future, so that they may take hold of the life which is life indeed" (I Tim. 6 : 18-19). In other words, St Paul says wealth can also serve the purposes of the Kingdom of God. In our opinion, this does not contradict the basic orientations of the Jerusalem community, but emphasizes different aspects. The redemption of wealth, and money in particular, does not mean submission to it, but its use in accordance with the demands of justice laid down in the Gospel.

But there are other important facts to be taken into account. For example, "A study of the Pauline vocabulary produces amazing results: the typical Greek expressions for poverty, such as *endées*, *pénès* and even *ptôchos*, are completely absent from the letters of St Paul" [16], and P. Seidensticker adds: "This analysis of the Pauline texts reveals the surprising fact that the notion of 'poverty', understood as a state of need, is almost totally absent from Paul's thinking." [17] The texts where the epistle clearly uses the term *ptôchos* are Rom. 15 : 16 and Gal. 2 : 10. In both cases, he appears to refer to the members of the Jerusalem community: these are the "poor of the saints", a term which could hardly have been coined by St Paul. P. Seidensticker says it is rather "a self-definition of the Jerusalem community. It is part of the religious motivation for the spirituality of the poor in primitive Judaism. For Paul, it means nothing more than an honorary title." [18] This does not imply, though, that the socio-economic element of poverty is not present in the life of the Jerusalem community. When the Epistle to the Galatians and even more the Epistle to the Romans were written, many years had passed since the Jerusalem community began to practise the common ownership of goods. At that time, the poverty which was at first overcome by the practice of *koinonía* at all levels must have reappeared. So the collection was also for those who lived in need, and not only those who were aware of being spiritually poor.

It is interesting to point out here that Paul never put forward the Jerusalem community as a model to be imitated, but as a group of believers who were to be helped. Writing to the Corinthians (II Cor. 8) on the problems relating to assistance, Paul does not say they should imitate Christ's example of "poverty" but "the gift" *(charis)* of Christ, who gives himself in love which enriches others. If the collection for the "poor of Jerusalem" has a meaning, it is that this is a way of removing the inequalities in the body of Christ: all parts, although in different places and having different functions, are equal and necessary since they are subject to the dominion of the Lord.

Moreover, it seems clear from P. Seidensticker's judgment that St Paul does not give priority to help for the needy: "We have no evidence of organized help for the poor in the Pauline communities such as is found in the first community of Jerusalem (Acts 6). Even less can we find any evidence of attempts to organize the community of goods on the basis of Christian charity (cf. Acts 2 : 4 ff.; 4 : 32-37; 5 : 1-11). We do not know, either, what were the exact functions of the "deacons" of Philippi (Phil. 1 : 1; cf. Rom. 12 : 7) and 'our sister, Phoebe,' a deaconess of the church at Cenchreae (Rom. 16 : 1). We only know the titles given to them, and conclude (mistakenly) that these people were responsible for 'serving at table'. However, there is no indication in the Pauline communities of any practice analogous to that known in the community in Jerusalem, according to the book of Acts. Neither do we know whether, or to what point, the 'Lord's Supper' served to assist the poor (cf. I Cor. 11 : 21). In any case, Paul does not pay special attention to the poor." [19] Consequently, the accent is placed on the body of Christ, not on the communion of goods. But we must repeat that, for the apostle to the Gentiles, the important thing was the exercise of brotherly charity, and this certainly would to some extent imply an active disposition towards the practice of charity within the Church, since the members of the same body, the same community, were to take care of each other (I Cor. 12 : 26; cf. 11 : 18 ff.). Continuing along this line of thought, we can say that within the Church there should be no needy, not even any poor, for, if the unity of the Church is based on brotherly love, which presumes the equality of all members of Christ's body, anything which tends to create tensions, divisions or rivalry, whether for social, economic or any other reasons, should be fought and overcome. Here our argument concurs with the writing of the Apostle Paul, true messenger of the unity of the Church and of brotherly charity.

A theology of poverty

Having said that, we must also say that Paul's thinking contains elements which allow us to outline what has been called "a theology of poverty". The fact that these elements are scattered and offer only the barest suggestions shows, again, that the subject was not of prime importance for Paul. But to return to these suggestions, some of which we have mentioned at other points in this study. We should underline first of all the affirmation that God has chosen what is weak, poor and despised in the world (I Cor. 1 : 18-30). Secondly, the importance of imitating the gift of Christ, to share his attitude of self-humiliation and self-denial (Phil. 2 : 5-8; II Cor. 8 : 9). Thirdly, openness to and anticipation of the coming of the Kingdom of God, that is, the establishment of divine justice, based on love, which corrects the distortions caused by men's sin (I Cor. 7 : 17, 20, 24 ; I Thess. 4 : 11-12; II Thess. 3 : 7-10). Fourthly, some concrete elements which arise from St Paul's social practice: for example, he never allowed the community to support him financially; on the one hand, to avoid putting obstacles in the way of the proclamation of the Gospel (I Cor. 9 : 12 ff.) and on the other hand, because he was always aware of "being a servant of Christ" (Gal. 6 : 6; I Tim. 5 : 17; I Cor. 9 : 7, and others). In this theological sketch on poverty according to the guidelines suggested by St Paul, the determining factor is always what God has done *in Christ*. The problem of the poor and the challenge of poverty for the apostle to the Gentiles seem to be resolved *in Christ*. St Ambrose, inspired by the apostle, rightly says: "If anyone seeks to please everyone, let him seek what is useful to many and not only to himself, following the example of St Paul. This is what it means to conform oneself to Chirst, not desiring what is improper and not harming another to benefit oneself. Our Lord Jesus Christ, being God, humbled himself and took the form of man (Phil. 2 : 6-7), which He enriched with the virtues of his works. Would you dare to deprive those whom Christ protected, or neglect those whom Christ clothed? For this is what you do when you put your own interest before another's." [20]

To sum up our discussion on the thinking and action of St Paul: *first*, while the subject of poverty does not seem to be a matter of priority in the Pauline epistles, this is to a great extent due to the fact that it was not a grave problem at that time among the congregations which grew up as a result of the apostle's missionary work. This would explain the rare occurrence of the word "poor" in Paul's writings. *Second*, while money cannot save, it can at least be redeemed when it is placed at the service of the needs raised by the practice of brotherly community in the Church. *Third*, the believer must not allow himself to become the slave of riches, but should adopt an attitude of self-denial based on and nourished by the freedom of life *in Christ* in the Spirit. Thus, although he himself is in need, the apostle is able to say: "I can do all things in him who strengthens me" (Phil. 4 : 13). *Fourth*, Paul requires that every Christian should, as far as possible, meet his needs through his own work (I Thess. 4 : 12). In other words, he does not feel attracted to voluntary poverty. Here we should note, referring back to our opening comments in this chapter on the meaning of the terms "wealth" and "poverty" in the Roman world — in whose context the apostle's mission was carried out — that every worker (especially if he is a craftsman, who works with his hands) belongs to the class of the non-rich, the poor.

All this takes us some distance from the radical nature of Jesus' message in the Gospels. To quote Seidensticker once more: "Paul has sought and found his own way to define Christian life and resolve its problems. The rules of his morality arise from the pascal condition of the Christian who, in Jesus Christ, has become a 'new creature' (Gal. 3 : 27; Col. 3 : 11). And from this pascal reality of Christ, Paul draws the conclusions which determine the pascal life of the Christian. Faced with these 'riches of Christ', all worldly realities have to a certain extent ceased to exist." [21]

The Epistle of James

The direct message of this epistle brings us back to daily reality. By this, we do not mean that the thinking of the Apostle Paul led us away from it, but, just as the problem of poverty is not given priority, daily reality certainly does not occupy first place in his attention which is preoccupied with theological reflection on the cosmic and transcendental aspects of the Christian life, from which result the admonitory pages of his epistles. But, in the text of James, we are confronted directly with the problems of ordinary people of the time. These pages were certainly written towards the end of the first generation of believers and the beginning of the second. At that time, the problem of the relationship between rich and poor in the life of the Church was becoming more apparent. Some took advantage of others (as usually happens), while the latter could only just contain their protests. Under these conditions, it is not surprising that James spoke out so strongly against the rich; this indicates that the problem was not avoided, but squarely faced, in the communities in which the texts were written. In James, the poor are the *pénès*; the wretched, the weak and oppressed, of low social standing, who are easily exploited and persecuted (such as, widows, orphans and slaves).

They are the ones who can lose nothing in this world, for they have nothing. But, they are also the ones who have everything to hope for in their poverty, hence their anxious expectations of the Kingdom of God. "James' contemporaries — without any doubt — were more familiar than we are today with this theological conception of poverty which must have been well known to them through the Psalms (cf. Ps. 22 : 25-27; 69 : 34), and the books of the prophets. In Isaiah, for example, we read that the shoot which is to come forth from the root of Jesse (that is, the Messiah who is expected to come in the future) will not judge according to appearances, but will bring justice to the poor and 'decide with equity for the meek of the earth' (Isa. 11 : 3-4; cf. also Isa. 58 and Mal. 3 : 5)." We can add that He will act, as St Matthew says (5 : 3 ff.) on behalf of the humble and merciful, and those who in general are not now treated with justice. This will be the miracle of the end of time: the poor shall be rich and will inherit the Promised Land; strength will grow up in the heart of the afflicted, the lame will leap like the hart, and grass will spring up in the desert (Isa 35). "Naturally, this marvellous hope was taken up again in the New Testament. Luke and Matthew both see in Jesus the beginning of the fulfilment of the old prophecy; hence the proclamation of the blessings which the Lord promised to the poor when the Kingdom should come: 'Blessed are you that hunger now, for you shall be satisfied. Blessed are you that weep now, for you shall laugh' (Luke 6 : 21)." [22]

The expectations of these humble people must have been so strong, and their material needs so great, that the author of the Epistle feels compelled to take their part and challenge the Christian community, some of whom say they follow Christ (who, in his call to men and women of his time to be his disciples, had emphasized the need to give a sign of their faithfulness to him through the rejection of material wealth) but nevertheless preserve odious social differences. What concerns the author of the text, then, is the lack of coherence among those who claim to believe, but do not direct their lives accordingly. This is what James means by those of "double mind", the *dipsychoi:*

those who, in the community which proclaims the justice of God, still live as friends of the old world already overcome by Christ.

"God destines the poor to be 'heirs of the Kingdom' (2 : 5). It is therefore in keeping with the will of God 'to visit orphans and widows in their affliction' (1 : 27). He who tries to win the favours of the rich, giving them the best places in the assembly and leaving the poor to 'sit at (his) feet' (2 : 3), is guilty of being a friend of the world and therefore an enemy of God. As for the rich, all their efforts to gain more profit and satisfy their passions will 'fade away' (1 : 11; 4 : 13; 4 : 3). Decomposition, rust, and fire will reduce their possessions to nothing (5 : 1-2). Their lives will bring them only tension, conflict and injustice (4 : 1 ff; 5 : 4). And their hearts which have no pity for others because they are 'fattened in a day of slaughter' can only lead them to ruin." [23]

Does this mean that the author of the Epistle of James exalts the poor? Not exactly, but he states that the Christian should respect the poor and behave justly towards them in accordance with the hope which opens the hearts of the people of God towards the future and leads them to live in an attitude of brotherly love and mercy. "My brethren, show no partiality as you hold the faith of our Lord Jesus Christ, the Lord of glory. For if a man with gold rings and in fine clothing comes into your assembly, and a poor man in shabby clothing also comes in, and you pay attention to the one who wears the fine clothing and say, 'Have a seat here, please,' while you say to the poor man, 'Stand there', or, 'Sit at my feet', have you not made distinctions among yourselves, and become judges with evil thoughts? Listen, my beloved brethen. Has not God chosen those who are poor in the world to be rich in faith and heirs of the Kingdom which He has promised to those who love him? But you have dishonoured the poor man. Is it not the rich who oppress you, is it not they who drag you into court? Is it not they who blaspheme that honourable name by which you are called?

"If you really fulfil the royal law, according to the scripture, 'You shall love your neighbour as yourself', you do well. But if you show partiality, you commit sin, and are convicted by the law as transgressors. For whoever keeps the whole law but fails in one point has become guilty of all of it. For He who said, 'Do not commit adultery', said also, 'Do not kill.' If you do not commit adultery but do kill, you have become a transgressor of the law. So speak and so act as those who are to be judged under the law of liberty. For judgment is without mercy to one who has shown no mercy: yet mercy triumphs over judgment" (James 2 : 1-13).

James takes a stance on behalf of the poor because he associates himself with the tradition of the whole people of God, throughout which Yahweh was always on the side of the humble. The Lord's judgment is very different from the judgment of the rich, who are always ready to accumulate and exercise power, which prevents them from having mercy and practising brotherly love. The justice of the Kingdom, outlined from the time of the choosing of Israel up to the sending of the Son of God to the world, was always with the needy, the weak, the unhappy and unfortunate. God's action in history is to repair the injustice of the rich and powerful. So how can there be social differentiations within the Christian community? How can the Church, the sign of the Kingdom which is to come, herald of the new day, maintain within it relationships marked by unjust social stratifications? This would be to ignore the Lord's words, echoed by James: "The poor shall be heirs of the Kingdom". James seems to react against these deviations, emphasizing that the faithful must love the poor. His text can be considered, then, as a teaching to the faithful in the form of warnings and guidelines aimed at encouraging Christians to live and carry out true piety. His attention to the poor is like an echo of Jesus' words in Matthew 25 : 31-46, which we have already mentioned. For James, the ethics of service and love are closely linked with the eschatological expectation of the Kingdom of God (see James 4 : 12 and 5 : 7 ff.).

In contrast to the direction of the teachings offered by the author of this text, the rich man enjoys what he has, guarding his possessions, dominated by them, and subjecting all other things to the demands of the administration of his capital. James condemns him for this, especially at the beginning of chapter 5: He is condemning the rich, and declaring that the End is at hand, which not only terminates their cupidity and enjoyment of it, but is a divine punishment upon them. There is a definite eschatological note in the warning. The thought of verse 2 was familiar enough; to quote Ben Sirac again: "*Wilt thou not leave thy wealth to another and thy labour to them that cast the lot ?... All flesh withereth like a garment, and the eternal decree is 'Thou shalt surely die'* (Ecclus. 14 : 15-17)." To which E. C. Blackman adds: "But James has more to say than that riches cannot be enjoyed for ever; the rich whom he is denouncing are told that they will not even be left to enjoy their ill-gotten gains for the normal span of life, for God's judgment on them is imminent. The 'last days' are almost here (5 : 3 to end)." [24]

This condemnation indicates that the author of the Epistle assumes that it is difficult for the rich to become Christians. It is the rich as an entire social group who are judged so harshly by this passage. Jesus had said that man could not serve two masters. For the grave error of the rich is to have a divided heart (if they claim to be part of the Christian community), even going so far as to deny Jesus (cf. I Cor. 12 : 3, those who called Jesus "cursed"). James is mainly concerned with the situation of the former, the *dipsychoi*, who behave "like a wave of the sea that is driven and tossed by the wind". These people claim to be part of the community of faith. Their double-mindedness constitutes a certain danger for the life of the people of God, since, in the end, they will act as a "counter-power" to the Lord, opposing the Spirit of God. It is these *dipsychoi* who practise unfair discrimination, and thereby threaten the equality which should exist between all the members of Christ's body. The social differences they represent are introduced along with them into the community of faith. They cause murmurings and jealousy among the people of God. This is why James urges: "Be doers of the word, and not hearers only" (1 : 22).

To sum up, the expectation of the justice of God and the Kingdom announced by Jesus motivates men to assist the poor, the weak, the orphan and the widow. By this means they practise and not only proclaim the word — true faith, true piety. This means taking the side of the needy, but also confronting the oppressors who are a real danger to the people of God. The rich and the oppressors are the enemies of the Lord for, even if they do not realize it, their hearts are divided. They practise unfair discrimination, their hearts are given to what is transient. Therefore, like the things they own, which are today but tomorrow will cease to be, they too will be ruined. Hence within the community of believers there must not be any of the social divisions which exist in the "world": judgment must go hand in hand with mercy and unpretentious love for one's neighbour.

The examples analyzed in this chapter do not allow too much generalization of the practice and thinking of the churches of the first and second Christian generations relating to the challenge of the poor and poverty. One thing, however, stands out: a loving response to the poor is a form of witness to the justice of the God who was expected with the coming of the Kingdom. It meant experiencing the first fruits of the Kingdom amid the old world. It was the reply of the people of faith to the friends of the world, the real "enemies of God" (James 4 : 4).

NOTES:

1 Cf. EDUARD SCHWEIZER: "La Comunidad de Siria", in *La Iglesia Primitiva, Medio Ambiente, Organización y Culto*, p. 33 ff. Salamanca: Ed. Sígueme, 1974.

2 P. SEIDENSTICKER: "St Paul et la Pauvreté", in *La Pauvreté Evangélique*, p. 94. Paris: Ed. du Cerf, 1971.

3 SERGIO ROSTAGNO: *Essays on the New Testament*, p. 42. Geneva: WSCF, 1976.

4 Dom HENRI LECLERC: *La Vie Chrétienne Primitive*, p. 21. Paris: Ed. Rieder, 1928.

5 ERNST TROELTSCH: *The Social Teaching of the Christian Churches*, Vol. I, p. 51. London: George Allen & Unwin; New York: Macmillan Co., third impression, 1950.

6 HANS LIETZMANN: *A History of the Early Church*, pp. 62-63. London: Lutter-worth Press, second impression, 1963.

7 J. DUPONT: "Les Pauvres et la Pauvreté dans les Evangiles et les Actes", in *La Pauvreté Evangélique*, p. 41, *op. cit.*

8 *Ibid.*, pp. 44-45.

9 *Ibid.*, p. 44.

10 R. MINNERATH: *Les Chrétiens et le Monde (1er et 2e Siècles)*, pp. 292-293. Paris: Gabalda, 1973.

11 St JOHN CHRYSOSTOMOS: *Sobre la Caridad Perfecta*, MPG, T. LVI, Col. 279.

12 MAURICE GOGUEL: *Les Premiers Temps de l'Eglise*, p. 60. Neuchâtel and Paris: Delachaux et Niestlé, 1949.

13 Cf. MAURICE GOGUEL: p. 61, *op. cit.*: "On trouve cependant quelques récits qui paraissent supposer une conception non autoritaire, mais démocratique de l'Eglise. Quand il s'agit de donner un successeur à Judas ou d'instituer le ministère des Sept, c'est l'assemblée des fidèles qui se prononce sur une proposition faite par Pierre au nom des Douze. En plusieurs endroits du livre des Actes (11 : 30; 15: passim; 16 : 4; 21 : 18), il est question d'Anciens ou de Presbytres sans que d'ailleurs, on puisse se représenter ni la manière dont ils se recrutaient, ni quel était leur rôle. Il n'est pas exclu que ce livre des Actes dit des Presbytres ou Anciens dans l'Eglise de Jérusalem ne soit que le reflet de ce qui existait dans les Eglises helléniques au temps où le livre a été rédigé. »

14 ERNST TROELTSCH: p. 63, *op. cit.*

15 MAURICE GOGUEL: says (p. 100, *op. cit.*) that it is not even a condition, but a request (today, we would say a "recommendation").

16 P. SEIDENSTICKER: p. 99, *op. cit.*

17 *Ibid.*, p. 102.

18 *Ibid.*, p. 106.

19 *Ibid.*, p. 114.

20 St AMBROSE: *Sobre los Deberes de los Ministros*, MPL, T. XVI, Col. 158.

21 P. SEIDENSTICKER: pp. 131-133, *op. cit.*

22 HELGA RUSCHE: *L'Epître de Saint Jacques*, p. 37. Le Pury & Lyon: Ed. Xavier Maffrus, 1967.

23 *Ibid.*, p. 116.

24 E. C. BLACKMAN: *The Epistle of James*, p. 141. London, S.C.M Press, 1957.

5 · Radical Demands and Disparate Behaviour

As we saw in the previous chapter in our analysis of the Epistle of James, the second generation of Christian believers was clearly composed of people from different social classes. This was inevitable because of the attraction of the Christian message for people of all backgrounds in the Mediterranean world of that time. The writer's stance in favour of the poor was a warning against the implications of the changes which he believed would probably come about in the Church owing to this social pluralism, and an attempt to preserve the radical nature of the gospel message. But we should not conclude from this that the communities of believers opened their doors to the influx of the rich without protest. Other New Testament writings also encouraged an attitude of vigilance to the dangers of wealth, though less radically than James. For example, in the Epistle to the Ephesians attachment to money is considered a form of idolatry, and avarice is as unworthy of the heirs of the Kingdom as fornication and impurity (Eph. 5 : 5).

Love of wealth should not be found among church leaders; the elders, for example, should be above reproach, avoiding the temptation of "shameful gain" (I Peter 5 : 2). The pastoral epistles also insist on this; the bishops should not be miserly (I Tim. 3 : 2-3) or "greedy for gain" (Titus 1 : 7). In fact, the warnings against the love of money were not only addressed to the church ministers responsible for the administration of the finances of the various communities, but they demonstrated the firm conviction of the faithful that love of money was incompatible with the foundations of the faith. The writer of the Epistle to the Hebrews exhorted his readers to be content with what they had, along the same lines that Jesus had indicated in his Sermon on the Mount (Matt. 6 : 25-34): "Keep your life free from love of money, and be content with what you have; for

he has said, 'I will never fail you nor forsake you' " (Heb. 13 : 5).
Even more clear is the author of the first Epistle to Timothy: "If any
one teaches otherwise and does not agree with the sound words of our
Lord Jesus Christ and the teaching which accords with godliness, he
is puffed up with conceit, he knows nothing; he has a morbid craving
for controversy and for disputes about words, which produce envy,
dissension, slander, base suspicions, and wrangling among men who
are depraved in mind and bereft of the truth, imagining that godliness
is a means of gain. There is great gain in godliness with contentment:
for we brought nothing into the world, and we cannot take anything
out of the world; but if we have food and clothing, with these we
shall be content" (I Tim. 6 : 3-8).

This attitude can also be detected in other writings more or less
contemporary with the New Testament canon, written in the period
of the transition between the second and third generations of believers,
and also in those written immediately afterwards. For example, the
Shepherd of Hermas shows the undeniable influence of the thinking of
James. For the *Shepherd*, poverty is an evil: "To those who can do
good, tell them to continue doing so, for it is beneficial for them to
do good works. For my part, I want them to know that every man
must be freed from his needs. For he who is in need and poverty
in his daily life is in great torment and anxiety. Thus he who frees the
soul of such a man from his need attains great joy for himself. He
who suffers such calamity undergoes the same torment and torture
as a man in prison. The fact is that many, unable to bear such misfortune, take their own lives. Hence he who knows the suffering
of such a man and does not free him from it commits a grave sin and
is guilty of his blood." [1] The author of this text sees in the lack of
solidarity with the humble a sign of unfaithfulness to the Lord who
calls us to live in brotherly love. It is a question of his redemption
and our own, and is therefore, a matter of great importance in the
preaching of the message of Christian love.

Hermas goes even further: he not only calls for brotherly charity,
but also gives a warning to those who risk losing their faith in the
Lord through their materialistic interests. At that time, Christians
had begun to suffer the misery of persecution and, when it came to
the test, some chose to deny the Lord rather than lose their wealth.
So the Shepherd says to Hermas: "Listen: there are those who have
never sought to examine the truth, nor to understand divine things,
but are content with a superficial faith and are submerged in business

dealings, wealth, friendships with the Gentiles and many other things of this world. All who are slaves to these vanities are incapable of understanding the allegories of the divine things, for their occupations blind them, ruin them, take away their life." [2] To this, he adds "the image of the building of the tower which represents the Church mentions the white, round stones which are not suitable for use in the construction. They are not rejected, but put on one side. These stones represent those believers whose wealth leads them to deny their faith when they are faced with persecution. They cannot be used until they have been re-shaped and something has been taken away from them. That something is their wealth." [3]

At this time, then, there was still a clear awareness that men had to choose between their faith and their wealth. It was not stated in the same radical terms as in the Synoptic Gospels or the Epistle of James, but the attitude persisted. It can also be seen in the *Didaché* which, following the tradition of the Gospel of St. Matthew and the beatitudes (presumably this text was written in the socio-cultural context of the Syrian Christian communities, where this Gospel may also have originated), advises: "You shall not seek your own elevation nor let your heart be led by insolence. You shall not bind your life to the world of the great, but shall walk the path of the righteous and the humble. You shall receive the events of your life as if they were goods, knowing that God is not removed from what happens." [4] The text mentions three dangers which threaten the life of the believer: the first is interior to the spirit of each person. The second concerns the milieu. And the third can appear in the daily happenings of life. The first danger is over-ambition, the aspiration to have what is not ours: power, and the excessive accumulation of possessions, which can only be achieved through dissension, hate and injustice. It is the very opposite of being the "poor of Yahweh", so well represented by Mary, "the handmaiden of the Lord", whose song of gratitude to God expresses her humility, her openness to divine action, her hope.

The second danger is the influence of this world, where the justice of God and the expression of his love are rejected. The road we are to take is that of poverty, persevering in justice and righteousness. Lastly, we must beware of the scepticism which can arise when our dearest and deepest hopes are not fulfilled; there are times when we are so disheartened because the justice of the Kingdom is not triumphant and we see the unjust receive rewards which they do not deserve, that we are tempted to abandon both hope and justice, surrendering to the powers of the world. The author of the *Didaché* emphasizes that the poor must not give up hope (for justice, for love which will reign over the hatred and social differences of today) when faced with suffering.

With all these warnings not to succumb to the temptation of wealth, the Church inevitably continued to attract the meek. Those who shared the life style of the rich and powerful in the Roman Empire necessarily scorned the believers and Christianity — Celsus, for example, whose disdain is clear from the way he speaks of the followers of Jesus Christ as people of low social condition, craftsmen who worked at the looms, cobblers, cleaners, slaves, and so on. The poor, at least, must have found in the Church a response to their deepest spiritual needs, but also their material needs. Some probably took advantage of it, and the *Didaché*, in its instructions on providing hospitality, indirectly points out that it had to be controlled in order to avoid the risk of unscrupulous persons doing no work at all, thanks to the generosity of the churches to whom they went asking to be received and sheltered. As Maurice Goguel says: "Charity in all its forms is no longer a spontaneous action in every case. It is the fulfilment of a duty; it is becoming organized. We are tempted to say it is becoming calculated." [5]

The rich enter the Church

Be that as it may, the rich gradually accepted the Christian faith, and wealthy people from the highest levels of Roman society were converted to Christianity. The words of I Peter 3 : 1-3, instructing women not to overindulge in luxurious clothes and complicated hairstyles, indicate that the Christian faith had reached the world of the rich and the information available about the persecution which took place under Domitian confirms this, for it shows that Christianity had made ground in the highest circles of Rome, even among those connected with the Emperor's family.[6]

This process, which must have become more marked towards the end of the first century and the beginning of the second, gradually led to a controversy which would have been unthinkable among the faithful of the first decades after the resurrection of Jesus Christ, when his demands were still very much alive in the minds of his followers: can the rich be saved while they are still rich, without giving up their possessions? A degree of compromise with wealth began to take shape; towards the end of the first century, Clement of Rome had begun to suggest that it was not necessary to renounce worldly possessions in order to be faithful to Jesus Christ; as Ernst Troeltsch says: "The only work which deals with the problem directly is — as is well known — that of Clement: *Can a Rich Man be Saved?*

"It is an allegorical account of the story of the rich young ruler, which suggests that it is not necessary to renounce possessions, but the spirit which clings to possessions; otherwise wealth ought to be used fully for the purposes of charity. It is most favourable towards wealth, and, at the same time, it is one of the most sensible works from the economic point of view and it is filled with tender piety." [7] But this was not a definite starting point for the compromise between the demands of the faith and the goods of this world. What concerned Clement was the salvation of men and women, including the rich, and how it is possible for the well-off to be converted to Jesus Christ in spite of their social condition. On the other hand, he believed (together with St Paul, whose position we have already discussed) that possessions can contribute to a more effective fulfilment of the demands of brotherly charity.

The well-known text of the Epistle to Diognetus, which describes in general but very moving terms the Christian life of the first decades of the second century, suggests, despite Clement's writings, that several centuries later the Christian community was still composed mainly of people from the less privileged sectors of society. "They are unknown, and yet they are condemned; they are put to death, and yet they give proof of new life. They are poor, and yet they make many rich; they lack everything, and yet in everything they abound. They are dishonoured, and yet their dishonour becomes their glory; they are reviled, and yet they are vindicated. They are abused, and they bless; they are insulted, and they repay insult with honour. They do good, and are punished as evildoers; and in their punishment, they rejoice as finding new life therein. The Jews war against them as aliens; the Greeks persecute them; and yet they that hate them can state no ground for their enmity." [8]

In any case, the problem raised by the growing presence of the rich in the Church was inevitable. The social homogeneity of the Christian congregations became less and less evident, and the difference between rich and poor heightened a discussion which, as we have seen, had begun around the end of the first century. Faced with the position of Clement, who was ready to accept a certain amount of luxury within the limits of what might be considered a normal life, Tertullian began to adopt a more rigid position. The teachings of Jesus, the experience of the Jerusalem community and the congregations founded by Paul, as well as the practice reflected in the Epistle of James, began to lose their concrete content as expressions of the faith which responded to very precise circumstances and situations. So the gospel precepts were considered as the norms, the expressions of a mandate which could not be neglected. In other words, confronted with the Church's success with the well-off, which suggests that the powerful and their customs in turn penetrated the life of the Christian congregations, the response of some was theoretical and prescriptive rather than realistic and adequate to the circumstances. Perhaps this was the most acceptable procedure for those who sought to defend the evangelical tradition by affirming their position. Faced with the problem raised by the presence of the rich in the Church, "Jesus' radical commandment of love was now emphasized in an abstract manner; the instructions to missionaries were turned into universal dogmas, and the story of the young ruler was made the basis of the system. The ascetic basis was quickened by the spirit of love, and the coarsening of the gospel morality of spirit and temper into the morality of the good works exalts individual deeds of sacrifice. The renunciation of possessions now becomes the main demand, whether it be from obedience to the commandment of love, which urges that no one ought to possess anything for himself so long as others are in want, or whether the ascetic idea is preeminent, that every joy in possession is self-love and love of the world and a hindrance to the love of God, or whether the sin-expiating power of almsgiving is emphasized. All along, however, private property itself remains untouched, but it is limited to the absolutely necessary minimum of existence; all that is superfluous must be given away." [9] This rigidity which Troeltsch describes as characteristic of the controversy surrounding the presence of the rich in the Church and all it implies can be seen in the following quotation from Tertullian, which is as cutting as the spirit of its writer who was so unwilling to accept differences and to be open to variations of existence: "If anyone is worried by the loss of his family possessions, we advise him, as do many biblical texts, to scorn worldly things. There can be no better exhortation to the abandonment of wealth than the example of Jesus Christ, who had no material possessions. He always defended the poor and condemned the rich." [10]

Because of the way the problem was raised, it also led to discussion about the relationship of the law to the Gospel. The text from Tertullian shows how what Paul considered an indication of "following the way of life of Christ Jesus" was understood in the second century as the requirement to follow "the example of Jesus Christ". Here, we seem to have entered the sphere of the law, of obligations. This is a long way, then, from the existential challenge of "*God or Mammon*", which can only be met from the depths of the human heart, which pledges its whole life in that response. So the witness of faith becomes an obligation, losing the dimension of freedom characteristic of those who live in the sphere of grace. It is not a matter of obligations or the imposition of models, but rather of behaviour based on neighbourly love and faithfulness to the Lord alone.

However, we would be wrong to think that dogmatic definitions of this kind prevented deep spiritual experiences through which the practice of brotherly charity and justice could be expressed in the churches of the time. Speaking of them some centuries later, St John Chrysostomos could say, "in the churches of that time, there developed a marvellous practice when all the faithful met together, after hearing the divine word, after the prayers and the communion of the mysteries, after the liturgical meeting; they did not return immediately to their homes, but the rich, who had prepared food and drink, invited the poor and set a common table, a common feast, a common invitation in the church itself, *so that the community of the table, and the piety of the place and a thousand and one other circumstances joined to make charity very close;* their pleasure was great and so was their gain. This practice was the source of countless benefits — the main one being friendship — becoming daily more warm after each liturgical meeting, since benefactors and beneficiaries felt united by such great love." [11] In other words, the eucharistic community is expressed not only through the liturgy, but also through the practice of brotherly love, by means of which social injustices are erased, or at least reduced.

The synthesis of the late second century

From what we can gather from the documents at our disposal, no one could (nor can now, in faithfulness to the gospel texts) question the priority which the practice of brotherly charity in the Christian community must give to the poor. Poverty (including in the period under review in this chapter) was still considered to be evil in the deepest sense of the word — not only socially, but also theologically and spiritually. However, this radical vision was not applied to dealings with those who were rich and powerful. The formidable admonitions of James and the existential challenge posed by Jesus to those who sought to follow him as their Master can only be found in the hard line taken by Tertullian. It would seem that, as the rich came to the Church in greater numbers, the radicality of the Gospel was played down. Troeltsch, who is very helpful to our understanding of this period, says that "very different conditions were allowed according to social class; upon the whole a fair amount of permissive comfort was permitted; this fact throws a good deal of light upon the 'existence minimum' and the question of private property, quite apart from the fact that the tone of the exhortations shows that these ideals were not carried out very far into practice. How natural it seemed to possess property is revealed by the fact that even Tertullian, who was so austere a man, counsels against Christian women marrying pagans, in order that the husband, by threatening to denounce his wife, may not cause her to renounce her property. All insight into practical details reveals the way in which property was taken for granted; it was only in eloquent speech about love that it took a secondary place." [12]

This does not mean that brotherly charity was not practised, but, contrary to our conclusions from our study of the communities recorded in the New Testament, in the second century charity is no longer directed so clearly towards the eradication of poverty, but towards opening people's minds to the implications of the spirit of love. In this sense, the practice of brotherly love fulfilled an educational role in the development of the Christian spirit. Service to the poor was seen as a way of deepening one's knowledge of God. Evidently, this service did lead to solidarity with the poor, reflected principally in the life style of the Christians of the time, who were generally comfortably off. "The spirit of restraint and simplicity of life are not to be given up; rather this spirit ought to be encouraged both in those who give and in those who receive. Both almsgiving and the expressions of charity ought to be determined by this standard." [13] In other words, as this emphasis developed in the practice of charity which left the rich still rich and the poor dependent on them, the powerful began to feel the need to adopt a more moderate way of life. And, what is more important because of its consequences

through the monastic movement, some believers from these privileged groups felt called to increase their self-denial, to practise a
certain asceticism which came to be seen as a kind of penitence for
sins committed.[14]

In the next chapter, we shall consider the influence of the monastic
tradition on the Church in the third and fourth centuries. Here, we
should mention another fact as the Church of that time tried to
respond in many ways to the challenge of poverty and the poor by
means of the trends which we have been discussing, a tendency
emerged which still predominates within Christian communities
today. To put it simply, we might say that the plurality of responses
means that there are at least two levels at which the community of
faith responds to the challenge of poverty: while some Christians live
as ordinary believers and in one way or another come to a compromise between the demands of faith and the styles of life around them,
others attempt to give a more radical response, with no concessions
to context, thus trying to maintain the fundamental demands of faith.
As a result, we have on the one hand "ordinary" Christians and, on
the other, those who choose a monastic life; on the one hand, those
who believe they could continue to have property and wealth, and
on the other, those who abandon everything in their eagerness to be
absolutely faithful to the demands of the Gospel. This, we believe,
was the result of the synthesis which took place in the second half
of the second century between the problem of the presence of the
rich in the Church, and the challenge presented to it by the poor
and poverty. The two extremes came together in a compromise
concerning the way in which brotherly charity should be
practised.

Now, as Troeltsch has said, charity on its own cannot promote
processes of social reform which permit the eradication of poverty
and in any way help to restore justice. It may alleviate the situation
of the poor, it may reduce their suffering, but it cannot reach the
roots of the problem. At that time, as we know, the expectation of
the imminence of the Kingdom of God had diminished. The eschatological hope of the final fulfilment of God's promises had gradually
given way to a concept which held that eschatology was already
fulfilled. Thus the intention, will and desire to eradicate poverty
and live as a community of equals diminished.

A ruling class was formed within the Church: bishops, adminis-
trators, influential people; this happened not only in the Christian

community but increasingly in the society of the Roman empire. According to Troeltsch, this class did not encourage any radical change in the structures of society of the time: the poor continued to be dependent on these new powerful. The unjust social structure of the Roman Empire was not deeply influenced by the growing Church. Of course, Christian values and behaviour introduced some elements which, in time, improved the situation to some extent. But poverty still existed. "Outside of the charitable activity led by the bishop, carried out by numerous officials, combining the care of the poor in their own homes with that in institutions, the clergy had not very much scope. The bishop was supposed to feed daily with the poor, and he did so very often; the clergy too were to be poor and without ostentation, an example of self-sacrifice to others, and in a great many instances they lived up to this ideal. But the influence of Christian ideas on the imperial legislation was quite insignificant. In this direction, the new class achieved nothing (and perhaps it did not wish to achieve anything), beyond the extirpation of pagans and heretics and the gaining of privileges for the Church." [15]

In this context, the most radical attempt to challenge and change the established order was that adopted towards the end of the second century and throughout the third century by the monastic movement, which was a clear decision to "break with the world". The movement also began to experiment with certain methods of production which led to the abolishment of private property.[16] Asceticism, the rejection of property, attempts to draw up rules for community life, gradually began to influence the movement, which was to show itself in all its strength through the great preachers of the Christian message of the fourth century, almost all of whom were educated in the context of the work of the monastic communities. From its position on the margin of the life style of most ordinary Christians, the monastic movement could challenge the compromise between the radical demands of the Gospel and the acceptance of wealth which had been taking shape, and the various means by which it was expressed. From within this movement came great personalities who, particularly in the fourth century, were to respond to the challenge of the poor and poverty, and also the practice of brotherly charity, a sign which defined true piety and fidelity to the Lord. This meant a new link with the purest gospel tradition at that time.

64   Good News to the Poor

NOTES:

[1] HERMAS: *Comparaciones X*, chapter IV, No. 2-3. Madrid: Ed. BAC. Los Padres Apostólicos, 1965.

[2] Quoted by Dom HENRI LECLERC: in *La Vie Chrétienne Primitive*, pp. 44-45. Paris. Ed. Rieder, 1928.

[3] MAURICE GOGUEL: *Les Premiers Temps de l'Eglise*, p. 159 — referring to the third vision of *Hermas*, 6 : 5-7. Neuchâtel and Paris: Ed. Delachaux et Niestlé, 1949.

[4] JEAN-PAUL AUDET: *La Didaché — Instrucciones a los Apóstoles* (*La Doble Vía* 3 : 9-10), p. 324. Paris: Gabalda, 1958.

[5] MAURICE GOGUEL: p. 159, *op. cit.*

[6] *Ibid.*, pp. 152-153.

[7] ERNST TROELTSCH: *The Social Teaching of the Christian Churches*, Vol. I, p. 184. London: George Allen & Unwin ; New York: Macmillan Co., third impression, 1950.

[8] *Epistle to Diognetus*, 5 : 11-17, quoted by B. J. KIDD, DD: *Translations of Christian Literature — Documents Illustrative of the History of the Church*, p. 55. New York: Macmillan Co., 1933.

[9] ERNST TROELTSCH: p. 184, *op. cit.*

[10] TERTULLIAN: *Sobre la Paciencia*, MPL, T. I, Col. 1371.

[11] St JOHN CHRYSOSTOMOS: *Homilia sobre las Herejías*, MPG, T. LI, Col. 256.

[12] ERNST TROELTSCH: p. 184, *op. cit.*

[13] *Ibid.*, p. 134.

[14] *Ibid.*, p. 136.

[15] *Ibid.*, p. 139.

[16] *Ibid.*, p. 141.

6 · The Prophets of the Church in the Time of Constantine

The compromise between the gospel tradition relating to poverty and actual practice which began to appear towards the end of the first century and beginning of the second was not restricted to customs and attitudes towards the values of the ruling culture. Its clearest expression was through the decrees of Constantine (313 AD), and we owe much of our understanding of it to Theodosius, who completed the work begun by Constantine towards the end of the fourth century. As we know, the year 313 was decisive in European history.[1] Until that time, while some elements of the synthesis between church and society had been raised, the tendency had been to widen the gap between them. This was particularly evident in the development of the monastic movement, which was always ready to stand back from the values and guidelines for conduct developed in Roman society. In this context, and despite the firm stances adopted by a militant minority within the Church, there can be no doubt that the incipient association between church and empire necessarily affected the Church in relation to the problem we are studying. On the one hand, the compromise was expressed in the increasing readiness of Christians to accept the dominant social order, which can easily be seen when we remember that, as time passed, the number of Christians holding positions of responsibility in the official administration grew steadily. This would have been unthinkable if the radical opposition between the Church and the ruling culture had been maintained. But, on the other hand, this acceptance produced at least two responses within the Church which we must include here.

The first consisted in the reaffirmation of the demands of the Gospel. The second led to a development in the practice of organized charity. The two lines converged around the figure of the priest and, more particularly, the bishop. For example, according to St Ambrose, nothing could do more to ensure the community's appreciation of the priest than his charity towards people in difficulties, especially the needy; he was to ensure that they had enough food to keep them from starvation. Moreover, the bishop of Milan calls attention to the need to give special priority to what he sees as a very important service to those whom he calls "the poor who are ashamed", that is, those who were rich but had been ruined by socio-economic changes which often occurred in the Lower Empire, forcing them into misery and deprivation where once they had lived in comfort. These people, who were ashamed of their poverty and tried to hide it, should be helped as far as possible, said St Ambrose.[2] But the priest's charitable work should not be limited to these "poor who are ashamed": it must also extend to prisoners and all those who might fear the powerful, for example, those condemned to death, in whose defence the priest should be ready to plead.

Apart from generosity, St Ambrose also emphasized that charity should be practised with discernment. "We must not confuse generosity with prodigality. *The priest must be able to judge how to be liberal without exhausting the reserves on one case, but sharing them among all in need.* The search for vainglory must never replace the search for justice! If this happens, he will easily fall victim to imposters and swindlers who are legion. Many pretend to be poor. They come asking for alms which they do not need, just so they can walk the streets and do nothing. They wear ragged clothes. They disguise their true age so as to receive more. They pretend to be in debt, or claim to have been robbed. All this must be carefully checked, so that the poor man's money shall not end up in the swindler's pocket. In a word, the priest's generosity must lie exactly half way between thoughtless prodigality and meanness which might lead him to give the money of the faithful to the undeserving." [3]

Elsewhere, the bishop of Milan insisted on the need to ignore social differences in the Church, since God's justice makes no distinction between rich and poor. Herein lies the particular emphasis of St Ambrose concerning the problem of the poor and wealth: the determining element is God's justice as we know it in the Scriptures, and principally in Jesus Christ; hence the following quotation which is clearly an echo of the parables of the foolish rich man, and the rich man and Lazarus, in the Gospel: "A narrow piece of ground is sufficient at the moment of burial, for the poor as well as for the rich, and the earth which was never enough to satisfy the ambition of the rich now covers him completely. Nature makes no distinction between men, either in birth or in death. It creates both alike and receives them in the same way in the tomb. *Who can establish classes among the dead?* Dig up a grave and see if you can tell who is the rich man. Then dig up another tomb and see if you can recognize the needy. The only difference may well be that a lot more things have rotted around the rich man." [4] These quotations from the Latin Father clearly reveal the two lines we suggested: the organization of charity by the ministers of the Church, and the confirmation of the Gospel's demands concerning the justice of God and the importance of caring for the poor.

St Basil: A powerful voice

St Ambrose's position is not unique. Similar opinions can be found among most leaders of the Church (both Latin and Greek) of the time, and especially those who belonged to the monastic movement. The movement's influence on the Greek Fathers was undeniable, and they frequently denounced the unjust social order which made social inequality part of the system. Among the leading figures of the monastic movement in the Eastern Church was St Basil, known as the "the Great". A hermit theologian who was one of the leading Cappadocian Fathers, "Basil became the first great representative of the monastic ideal of the priest and the bishop, to whom the age that followed referred again and again. He soon became popular with the people of Caesarea. He created, no doubt very largely from his own resources, a whole complex of charitable welfare institutions. There arose a whole 'new city' (Greg. Naz. Or. 43, 63) grouped around the church and monastery, consisting of hostels, almshouse, and hospitals for infectious diseases, and the bishop himself took up residence there. The foundation was imitated and much admired, and also criticized. It was regarded as a threat to the State administration, an objection which Basil himself refused to accept. The spirit that inspired these works of charity was more monastic than political and hierarchic. It was not intended that the laity should sink back into passivity. Basil's sermons were full of practical exhortations and examples, stimulating to acts of Christian love and the practice of virtue. Especially during the great famine of the year 368, he proved his mettle in impressive sermons against the profiteers and the indifferent rich. He himself organized free meals for the people which were also available to immigrant foreigners, pagans, and even the infidel children of Israel." [5] In more than one sense, St Basil's action and thinking can be seen as exemplary and characteristic of the monastic current among the Greek Fathers, so it would be useful to spend some time looking at his treatment of the problem.

In the first place, he saw wealth as "a good to be administered, and not a source of enjoyment: this should be the judgment of any healthy conscience". [6] The error lies in covetousness (cf. I Tim. 6 : 10), because it leads to all sorts of evils,[7] including — and not least — injustice: "What do I do wrong, you say, in admiring what is mine? Tell me what is yours. Who gave it to you to possess it for life? It is as if someone who pays for a seat in the theatre then chooses the others who may attend, claiming to own the theatre, when in fact it is for the use of all. This is what the rich do: since they are the first to occupy a common good, they think they are entitled to take it for themselves. If each one were content with what is necessary, and left the rest to the needy, there would be neither rich nor poor. Were you not born of your mother's womb? Will you not likewise return naked to the earth? And from whom have you received the goods you now possess? If you answer 'from destiny' you are an infidel who refuses to recognize his creator and to give thanks to his benefactor. If you agree that you have received them from God, tell me why they have been given to you. Is God so unjust that he shares out unfairly the things that are necessary for life? Why have you got plenty while another lives in misery? Couldn't it be perhaps so that you will one day be rewarded for your goodness and faithful stewardship, while he receives his crown for his patience? But you, who pack all your belongings into the bottomless sack of your miserliness, who think you do no harm to anyone, are nevertheless robbing many of your fellow men.

"What is a miser? One who is not content with what is necessary. What is an exploiter? One who takes another's possessions. Aren't you a miser, a plunderer, when you use for your own benefit something which has been given to you to be administered? He who takes another's coat is a thief; do you deserve any other name if you do not help to clothe the naked? The bread which you keep for yourself although you do not need it belongs to the hungry; the cape hanging in your wardrobe should cover those whose clothes are in shreds; the shoes you spoil should be for those who are barefoot; in the same way, the money you have buried should be given to the needy.

You commit as many injustices as there are people with whom you avoid sharing what you have." [8]

Together with the injustice implicit in the undue accumulation of wealth, St Basil also criticizes irresponsible economic growth. On the basis of the parable of the foolish rich man (Luke 12 : 16-21), St Basil equates economic growth whose aim is the accumulation of wealth with human wickedness. In the homily on this subject, he clearly sees it as a sign of stupidity, covetousness, and evil, with all its injustices and lack of consideration for the poor and needy. "Indeed, you who will die some day, what are you thinking? *'I will pull down my barns, and build larger ones.'* You do well, I say in turn: your barns of iniquity deserve to be demolished. Destroy with your own hands what you have built for this evil purpose. Pull down those storerooms which have never helped anyone. Destroy this house where you keep the fruits of your avarice, demolish those roofs, bring down those walls, put the harvested wheat on the ground, free your wealth from the prison in which you have kept it, and let light shine into the shadowy caves of your fortune. *'I will pull down my barns, and build larger ones.'* And when these are full too, what do you think you will do? Destroy them again and build more new ones ? What could be more foolish than forever tiring yourself out, carefully building barns only to pull them down again? If you like, your barns could very well serve to house the poor. So harvest your treasure in heaven." [9]

The unfair accumulation of wealth by private individuals is, then, a form of injustice,[10] and there is a clear transgression of the divine will in the irresponsible use of wealth,[11] and submission to covetousness: "For the sake of wealth, relatives deny nature; brothers look at each other with the eyes of criminals; for the sake of wealth the deserts breed robbers, the seas breed pirates, the cities breed sycophants. Who is the father of untruth, who makes false accusations? Who begets perjury? Isn't it wealth and the desire to acquire it? What's the matter with you all ? Who turned your own goods into a snare to trap you? 'Wealth is an aid to life.' Perhaps money was given as an instrument of evil?" [12] Whoever gives in to the temptation of wealth shares in a system of oppression, since wherever he looks he will see only "the clear images of his crimes: here the tears of the orphan, there the groanings of the widow, the poor he has ill-treated, the slaves he has punished, the neighbours among whom he stirred up anger." [13]

For St Basil, the problem arises because we live in a system of injustice and exploitation from which the believer should dissociate himself while at the same time working for change. Otherwise God's judgment will fall upon those who, consciously or unconsciously, are in complicity with the system: "Fishes eat different food according to their species. Some eat mud, some eat algae, some eat the plants which live in the water. However, most of them eat their fellows, and the littlest is food for the biggest. And if the one that eats the smaller fish is in turn caught by a larger one still, both end up in the same stomach. And what are we men doing when we oppress the lower class? What is the difference between what the fish do and the man who, in his avid love for wealth, swallows up the weak? That man has seized what belonged to the poor; you, who robbed him in turn, made him part of your opulence. You have revealed yourself as the most wicked of the wicked and the most avaricious of the avaricious. Take care that you do not meet the same end as the fish: the hook, the rod or the net. For, if we behave like the wicked, we will not escape the final torture." [14] It can be seen, then, that for St Basil the condition of poverty is an evil, and reveals tremendous injustice, for it is the result of social exploitation. On this point, St Basil, like other Fathers of the time, as we shall see in a moment, concurs with the biblical and evangelical tradition. This destroys the notion that the monastic movement held poverty up as an ideal — at least at the time of Constantine's new approach to the Church and State.

This is corroborated by the writings of St Gregory of Nazianzus and St John Chrysostomos. The former, for example, always took a strong stand against the undue appropriation of material goods and the injustice it breeds, often opening the way to slavery.[15] He criticizes the moneylenders very harshly.[16] Chrysostomos, for his part, never tired in his prophetic denouncement of the exploitative system which prevailed at the time. For Chrysostomos, the priority is to love justice and train oneself to seek only what is just and necessary, for only thus can one fight against all forms of social injustice wherever it is found. It is important to emphasize that Chrysostomos, who was Patriarch of Constantinople towards the end of the fourth century and beginning of the fifth, was against the system in which both poor and rich participate. The poor who try to emulate the rich are also guilty of injustice; they are trapped by the system: "Enough of stealing what is not yours, both rich and poor; for now I am speaking not only to the rich but also to the poor. For the poor also rob those who are poorer than they; the richer and stronger craftsmen exploit the more needy and less well off; the tradesmen exploit other tradesmen, and those who sell in the market. I want to eradicate injustice everywhere. An unjust act is not measured according to the amount defrauded or stolen, but by the intention of the one who robbed or defrauded. This is true, and I remember saying to you that the most miserly and the thieves are those who do not forgive even small amounts, and I think you, too, will remember this... Let us learn not to want more than is fair and not to covet what we do not need. In the things of heaven, our longing should not be limited: there, we should desire always more; but on earth, each one should seek only what is necessary and sufficient and not ask for more, so that we can obtain true goods through grace." [17]

But we should explain that in other passages in his extensive work, St John Chrysostomos does not place poor and rich on the same level. The injustice of the rich is greater, since their exploitation of the poor is a sign of a social injustice which is a blasphemy against the just will of God. Hence his hard words against the rich, which must have stung like whiplashes in the Court of Constantinople: "But let us leave these people, if they don't mind, and turn to others who seem no less unjust. Who are these others? Those who occupy the fields and extract the wealth of the land. Can anyone be more wicked than these men? If you look how they treat the brave but miserable labourers, you will see that they are more cruel than the barbarians. They make continual and unbearable demands on those who are wracked with hunger and spend their lives working, and force them to do the hardest work. They treat them like asses or mules, or rather like stone, and allow them not a moment's rest. Whether or not the land produces, they oppress them just the same, and pardon them nothing." [18]

The duty of the rich

The message of the Fathers to the faithful of the time indicates, among other things, that a person is never less valuable than his wealth, and that a human being cannot be judged solely by the goods he possesses. If anyone claims that he is greater because he owns more, he is guilty of a terrible confusion between being and having. True, no one can *be* without *having*, but it is a sad mistake if being is *equated* with having. Rather, one has in order to be. But one does not exist in order to have. When one lives to seek possessions, the meaning of human existence is terribly limited, and it is difficult to achieve the happiness which comes from the fulfilment of justice. St Augustine, in his *Commentaries on the Psalms*, gives an example of how the Latin Fathers, like the Greeks, criticized this abhorrence: "All men do whatever good or evil they do to free themselves from the causes of their misfortune and to acquire happiness, and they always seek to live happily, whether by good or evil. However, not all of them attain what they seek. Everyone wants to be happy, but only those who act justly will be happy. I don't understand how those who do evil can hope to be happy. How? By owning money, silver and gold, land, houses and slaves, by the pomp of this world and worldly honour which is fickle and transitory. They seek to find happiness by owning things.

"But what must you own to be happy? When you are happy, will you be better than you are now, wretched as you are? It is not possible for what is worse than you to make you better; you are a man, and everything you long for to make you happy is inferior to you. Gold and silver and any material thing you long to obtain, possess and enjoy are inferior to you. You are better and are worth more, and as you wish to be happy, you want to be better than you are because you are unhappy. True, it is better to be happy than wretched. But to be better than you are, you seek what is worse than you. Everything on earth is worse than you... So take my loyal advice: we all know you want to be better and we all want it too; seek what is better than you, which is the only thing that can make you better." [19]

Faithful to the message of Jesus, the Fathers call the rich to conversion, to abandon the love of wealth for the love of God. When this is accepted, men no longer seek to hoard goods, but begin to care for others, especially the least privileged. Riches save nobody; but the love of God, which compels us to love our neighbour, gives a fuller meaning to human existence. The thirst for riches, then, is incompatible with the Gospel." [20]

Again, St Basil emphasizes that the rich must repent, for the greater a man's wealth, the less perfect his charity, even though his behaviour (including his religious life) may seem very worthy: "Though you have not killed, like you say, nor committed adultery, nor stolen, nor borne false witness, you make all of this useless unless you add the only thing which can allow you to enter the Kingdom. Clearly you are far from that requirement (charity), and you are mistaken in claiming that you love your neighbour as yourself. If it is true that you have kept the law of charity from your childhood, as you claim, and that you have done as much for others as for yourself, then where does all your wealth come from? Care for the poor absorbs all available resources... So whoever loves his neighbour as himself owns no more than his neighbour does. But you have a great fortune. How can this be, unless you have put your own interests before those of others? The more abundant your wealth, the less perfect your charity. I know many people who fast, pray, groan, and do any kind of pious work that doesn't affect their pockets, but at the same time they give nothing to the needy. What good are their merits? The Kingdom of heaven is closed to them. Every time I go into the home of one of these foolish rich people, resplendent with ornaments, I notice that for its owner there is nothing more precious than visible goods, which deck him out according to his pleasure, but that he despises his soul. I wonder, then, what great benefit this silver furniture and ivory chairs can produce so that all these hoarded riches are not passed to the poor, who in their multitudes cry in misery at the gates of the rich men's houses." [21]

Wealth, then, is to be used sensibly, and this means using it to meet the needs of the poor. To put this in another way, the value of wealth depends on how far it is applied to helping the needy.[22] So riches exist to be shared. Material goods, as gifts from God, must be seen as common property, rather than being hoarded by individuals. "It is a sign of sickness and wickedness if the rich retain what they have for themselves, for this means their ruin, and the ruin of others. Whatever is put into your hands, do not keep it for yourselves alone, for you damage the common good; but before anyone else you damage yourselves. Don't you want anyone to share in your wealth? Then you must not share in anything that belongs to someone else. And, if this were to happen, there would be a universal upheaval. Wherever it may be, giving and taking is the source of many good things, be it seeds, disciples or arts. He who seeks to retain his art for himself alone ruins himself and upsets the whole of life." [23]

The requirement to practise charity is understood by these Fathers in terms almost as radical as those of Jesus' teachings in the Gospel: one must give what one has, and not what one has left over. "That is not almsgiving. Almsgiving is the action of the widow in the Gospel, who gave up all she had to live on (Mark 12 : 44)." [24] The problem of the rich man, the reason for the criticism against him, is that he is not prepared to give according to the needs of others, but only according to the demands of the love of riches which rules his life. By doing so, he reveals how materialistic his spirit is, which is the same as saying how merciless he is. "You have not been merciful, so you will not be shown mercy; you have not opened your doors, so those of the Kingdom of heaven will be closed to you; you have not given a piece of bread, so you will be refused eternal life." [25] By his negative response to the challenge of the poor, by refusing to fight against the patent injustice of poverty, the rich man responds negatively to the offer of the Kingdom of God and the Lordship of Christ; he shows that his soul is where his possessions are. So, if he is to receive the justice of the Kingdom, he must change; he must transform his existence, he must alter the direction of his whole life.

The rich man who undergoes this kind of conversion begins to share what he has with the poor for the sake of the Lord. "When you share with the poor for the sake of the Lord, you are making both a gift and a loan: a gift, because you do not expect repayment; a loan, because of the generosity of the Lord who will respond on behalf of the poor and who will give you ample compensation for the little you have given. Indeed, 'He who is kind to the poor lends to the Lord' (Prov. 19 : 17). Don't you want the Lord of all things to reimburse you? If a rich man from the city undertakes to pay for others, do you accept his guarantee or not? But you do not accept that God should stand guarantee for the poor! Give away the money which is useless to you, without charging interest; it will be a good thing for everyone. For you, it will ensure your capital; for the other, the benefit he makes from its use. If you still want any income, content yourself with what the Lord is keeping for you: he will pay you the interest of the poor. Expect true proofs of goodness from him who is truly good."[26]

The road to overcoming poverty

All this indicates that the Fathers of the Church during the empire of Constantine insisted, as do the Gospels, that the Christian must share what he has for, in so doing, he bears witness to the justice of God. The man of faith responds to the challenge of the poor in such a way that he shows himself to be a disciple of Jesus, the true "poor of Yahweh". The challenge of the poor is also faced when the believer (and the Church as the body of believers) struggles against social injustice, denounces its causes, and urges those who have the resources to prevent them from being used in this way. The Fathers put this challenge directly to the well-to-do of their time. Clearly, the rich had to be confronted with this message: as long as they continued to accumulate wealth, they were hurting the poor and so hurting Jesus.[27]

But the poor cannot overcome their condition by setting themselves to imitate the wealthy, or by placing their hopes only in the rich and their compassion for, by so doing, they simply confirm their dependence on the rich and powerful. The road the poor must take in their struggle against poverty is that of *self-reliance* in which they walk by trusting in the strength which each one receives from the Lord. " 'Drink water from your own cistern' (Prov. 5 : 15). In other words, consider your means, don't go begging from other sources, but seek your life's sustenance from your own resources. You have pots of bronze, clothes, a horse, some furniture. Sell them; accept anything, rather than lose your freedom. You may say it costs you dearly to sell them. Don't go knocking on other doors. 'The well of one's neighbour is always narrow.' It is much better to meet your needs through your own work than to be lifted up suddenly thanks to another's support, only to lose all your resources straight afterwards. If you have money to pay with, why not use your resources to relieve your misery? Do not submit yourself to the moneylender who will attack you, nor let yourself be hunted and captured like prey." [28]

The Fathers' message to the Christian community can be summarized as a call to practical solidarity and, here again, they concur with the demands of the Gospel, inspired by the book of Acts' accounts of the Jerusalem community.[29] This is their way of putting into practice Christ's mandate concerning brotherly love and the way He was to be served by helping the needy: "To conclude, if you believe what I say, servants of Christ, brothers and fellow heirs, while there is still time let us visit Christ, care for Christ, feed Christ, clothe Christ, welcome Christ, honour Christ; not only by seating him at our table, as some did (Luke 7 : 36); nor with ointments, like Mary (John 12 : 3); nor only with a burial, like Joseph of Arimathea; nor with what was needed for the burial, like Nicodemus, who only half loved Christ; nor with gold, incense and myrrh, like the wise men before all the others. No, the Lord of all things wants mercy rather than sacrifice (Matt. 9 : 13), and He wants hearts full of compassion rather than thousands of lambs; let us give them to him, then, through the poor and those who suffer today, so that when we leave this world we shall be received in the eternal storehouses by the same Christ our Lord, to whom be the glory for ever. Amen." [30] The rule of life which the Fathers suggest for the community of believers is inspired by the gospel records of how the disciples lived with Jesus, and the experience of the Christian community of Jerusalem. This inspiration is what later took shape in the monastic movement. This community of goods was to be a sign of the communion which should reign in the life of the Church: "The rule of perfect Christianity, its clearest definition, its highest peak, is *agreeing to seek the common good*. The apostle added: 'As I am of Christ' (I Cor. 11 : 1). And nothing can make us imitate Christ so well as caring for our neighbours. Though you fast, though you sleep on the hard ground, even though you give your life, unless you look towards your neighbour, you have done nothing much: despite all you have done, you are still a long way from this model." [31]

If there are riches to be gained, they are the spiritual and religious riches of Christ, as the Fathers said many times. Meanwhile, the Constantinian synthesis gave rise to other compromises: at the same time as the radical preaching in the Temple, or the life of radical sharing in the monasteries, most believers began to accept a compromise between faith and the values which prevailed in daily life. From that moment, especially from the beginning of the fifth century, the compromise led to two kinds of Christian life: on the one hand were those who tried to be faithful to the rigorous demands of the Gospel; on the other hand, those who tolerated a degree of compromise between Christian conduct and the dominant social system.

The contradiction between the two had to explode, but almost always resolved itself in favour of the system and established power. The case of St John Chrysostomos, who was twice expelled from Constantinople for taking an obviously prophetic stance in relation to the life-style of the imperial court, is a clear example. His death, truly the death of a poor man, is also a clear model of the strength with which the Fathers held fast to their convictions in their efforts to be faithful to Jesus Christ. However, in various ways, the Christian witness began to weaken within society in the last years of the Roman world. These two kinds of religious behaviour also tended towards the establishment of a dichotomy in the life of those believers who were most open to the prevailing culture and the social system which went with it. On the one side was the religious life (the level of the Temple, one might say), and on the other was property, power, business, the acceptance of the ambiguity of secular society.

To sum up, we would do well to quote Ernst Troeltsch's comments on how a solution was found to the problem of the acquisition of goods in the Church during the fourth century, that is, during the Constantinian period: "Above all, in a society constructed upon the census and on distractions based on wealth, the Fathers lay stress on the true and real classification of human beings according to the only effective 'riches', the riches of virtue and piety. They also point out that the true order or rank is independent of the social differences revealed by the census, which determined the right of being elected to city councils, and the possibility of belonging to the senate and the official classes. Here, the Christians appropriated for their own use similar powerful phrases of the Stoics. That this 'having property though one had it not' might lead just as easily to 'having Christianity as though one had it not' is obvious. All the more strongly, therefore, the other solution was emphasized — the way of monasticism. Here, the difficulty was removed by doing away with any private property altogether; the real motive for this, however, was no longer love but asceticism. But in the love exercised within the monastic community, and in intercession for those who are living in the world, love still comes into her own. Thus, the principle of a double morality, by means of which the Church solved the problem of the relationships between the world and the ethic of the Gospel, was also the solution of the problem of poverty." [32]

Clearly, this was no way to eradicate the poverty of the masses of the Empire, nor even of those who had been converted to Christianity. Unfortunately, it helped rather to consolidate the situation of inequality in society. This meant that there was a need to refine the means of helping the poor. The struggle to eradicate poverty as such ceased to exist, and was replaced by ways of alleviating the suffering of the poor. A large proportion of the Church's budget had to be set aside to help the poor, to be distributed among the victims of social evils; true, this did not always happen, since the bishops often kept most of the Church's money for their own use and that of their clergy. Witness this quotation from Henry Chadwick: "At Rome in the fifth century, a quarter of the revenue went to the bishop, while the remaining three quarters was equally divided between the remaining clergy, those on the official list of the sick and poor, and the maintenance of the church buildings. It was always recognized that the prime responsibility of the church treasury was to provide for the needs of the poor, and bishops who preferred to spend money on rich adornments and splendid churches were generally disapproved; in any event, there was no question of such elaboration before the time of Constantine." [33] This was the inevitable result of the acceptance of synthesis and compromise. This solution to the problem was to be decisive in the Church's response to the challenge of the poor and poverty in the centuries which followed. The intention was to relieve the suffering of the victims of injustice rather than to present a radical witness to the justice of God.

NOTES:

[1] Cf. CHARLES NORRIS COCHRANE: *Christianity and Classical Culture: A Study of Thought and Action from Augustus to Augustine*, p. 177 ff. London, New York and Toronto: Oxford University Press, 1944.

[2] Cf. R. GRYSON: *Le Prêtre selon St Ambrose*, p. 297. Louvain: Ed. Orientaliste, 1968.

[3] *Ibid.*, p. 301 (our emphasis).

[4] St AMBROSE: *Libro sobre Nabot de Yizreel*, MPL, T. XIV, Col. 707 (our emphasis).

[5] HANS VON CAMPENHAUSEN: *The Fathers of the Greek Church*, p. 86. New York: Pantheon Books, 1959. Cf. also Emilianos Timiadis: *Les Migrants*, pp. 127-205. Paris, Ed. SOS, 1971.

[6] St BASIL: *Homilías*, VII, 3, MPG, T. XXXI, Col. 288.

[7] In this respect, see also St JOHN CHRYSOSTOMOS in *Homilía sobre San Mateo*, MPG, T. LVIII, Col. 608: "Do not talk to me, then, of the abundance of riches. Consider, rather, the harm suffered by those who love them, for they lose heaven for their sake. It is as if a man who has lost the highest honour in the imperial palace is then puffed up with pride because he possesses a heap of dung. True, a heap of money is no better, or rather, dung is worth more than money. Dung serves at least to manure the fields, to heat water, and suchlike; gold which is buried beneath the earth cannot do any of this. If only it were just useless! But the truth is that it kindles many fires against him who possesses it and doesn't use it as he should, and infinite evil is born of it. This is why secular writers call covetousness a fortress and the blessed Paul, in better and more expressive words, calls it 'the root of all evil' (I Tim. 6 : 10)."

[8] St BASIL: *Homilías*, VI, 7, MPG, T. XXXI, Col. 276-277.

[9] St BASIL: *Homilías*, III, 6, MPG, T. XXXI, Col. 273-276.

[10] St JEROME also speaks very clearly on this point. Cf. *Cartas*, MPL, T. XXII, Col. 984: "The Gospel rightly calls riches 'unjust' because they have no origin other than injustice, and nobody can own them without another losing them.

I therefore believe the truth of the popular saying, 'The rich become rich through their own injustice and through good inherited unjustly from others'."

[11] See also St John Chrysostomos: *Homilia XIII sobre I Cor.*, MPG, T. LXI, Col. 113: "I say this not because wealth is a sin; no, the sin lies in not sharing it among the poor, in misusing it. Nothing God has made is evil; everything is very good. Therefore, wealth, too, is good, provided it does not dominate those who possess it and that they save their neighbours from their poverty."

[12] St Basil: *Homilia contra los Ricos*, MPG, T. XXXI, Col. 297.

[13] St Basil: *Homilia VII*, 6-7, MPG, T. XXXI, Col. 296-297.

[14] St Basil: *Homilia VI sobre el Hexámeron*, MPG, T. XXIX, Col. 152.

[15] St Gregory of Nazianzus: *Sobre el Eclesiastes*, MPG, T. XLIV, Col. 664.

[16] St Gregory of Nazianzus: *Contra los Usureros*, MPG, T. XLVI, Col. 435.

[17] St John Chrysostomos: *Homilia X sobre I Tesalonicenses*, MPG, T. LXII, Col. 462. In this respect, see also Zenon de Verona: *Tratado III sobre la Justicia*, MPL, T. II, Col. 286: "To avarice, we owe the fact that the granaries of some are full of wheat while the stomachs of many others are empty, and prices are raised owing to restricted supply. Avarice is responsible for fraud, plunder, disputes and war; it is responsible for striving for profit while others groan in misery; the confiscation of goods has become an industry; the appetite for others' goods cries out under pretext of self-defence, so that the defenceless and innocent lose what they have by law, which is worse than any violence. For what has been taken away by force can sometimes be recovered, but what has been taken away under the shelter of the law can not. Let him who wants to glory in this injustice; but he must know he who enriches himself on the misery of others is the most wretched of men."

[18] St John Chrysostomos: *Comentario sobre el Evangelio de San Mateo*, MPG, T. LVIII, Col. 591.

[19] St Augustine: *Comentario a los Salmos*, MPL, T. XXXVI, Col. 293.

[20] Cf. St Basil: *Homilia VII*, 2-5, MPG, T. XXXI, Col. 284-293.

[21] St Basil: *Homilia VII*, 1, 3 and 4, MPG, T. XXXI, Col. 280-281, 288, 289-292.

[22] Cf. St John Chrysostomos: *Comentario sobre el Evangelio de San Mateo*, MPG, T. LVIII, Col. 714 ff. See also Mario Miegge: *I Talenti Messi a Profito*, pp. 49-52. Urbino: Argalia Editore, 1969.

[23] St John Chrysostomos: *Homilia VIII sobre I Cor.*, MPG, T. LXI, Col. 86-87.

[24] St John Chrysostomos: *Sobre la Carta a los Hebreos*, MPG, T. LXIII, Col. 197.

[25] St Basil: *Homilia contra los Ricos*, MPG, T. XXXI, Col. 292.

[26] Cf. St Basil: *Homilia II sobre el Salmo XIV*, MPG, T. XXIX, Col. 263-280.

[27] St John Chrysostomos: *Homilia VIII sobre I Cor.*, MPG, T. LXI, Col. 94.

[28] St Basil: *Homilia II sobre el Salmo XIV*, MPG, T. XXIX, Col. 263-280.

[29] St Basil: *Homilia VIII*, 8, MPG, T. XXXI, Col. 325-328.

[30] St Gregory Nazianzus: *Sobre el Amor a los Pobres*, MPG, T. XXXV, Col. 909.

[31] St John Chrysostomos: *Homilia VIII sobre I Cor.*, MPG, T. LXI, Col. 208.

32 ERNST TROELTSCH: *The Social Teaching of the Christian Churches*, Vol. I, p. 118. London: George Allen & Unwin; New York: Macmillan Co., third impression, 1950.
33 HENRY CHADWICK: *The Early Church*, p. 57. Harmondsworth: Penguin Books, 1967.

7 · The Western Church in the Late Middle Ages

The "Sequela Christi" and the Practice of Charity

Since the nature of the challenge of the poor and poverty to the Church in the late Middle Ages is closely linked with the way in which they were treated in the first centuries of Christian history, it would be interesting at this point to take a look at the last four decades of the 12th century and the early decades of the 13th, a period of great richness in the evolution of the western Church. We cannot hope to do justice to the vast wealth of experience and spiritual life acquired during this period, but these years bring valuable elements to our analysis.

At that time, the great fear of the end of the first millennium had receded. The synthesis described in chapter 6 had produced huge problems for the Church: simony and the corruption of the clergy were frequent during the centuries of the high Middle Ages and the beginning of the late Middle Ages. However, the monasteries not only preserved the classical culture, but also, along with other minority sectors of the Church, maintained a tradition in which in one way or another the basic orientation given to Christian charity as assistance to the suffering, help to the needy, consolation to the mourners, was put into practice. In the eastern Church, this led to the organization of assistance centred around orphanages, hospitals, hostels, schools, and so on.[1] In the East as in the West, these responses to the various forms taken by the challenge to the Church resulted in close contact with secular institutions and especially the principalities and powers of the time. This was inevitable because of the conditions produced by the Constantinian synthesis.

But the synthesis did not imply complete harmony between the elements which composed it. While for a long time it was the secular arm of the Empire which was the determining factor in the process, often subjecting the spiritual arm to earthly authority, a reaction gradually took shape within the Church against it. It originated in the monastic movement in the West, which, towards the end of the 11th century, attempted a reform of the Church when Hildebrand was enthroned as Pope of Rome under the name Gregory VII. Some saw this as a great victory for monasticism in the West, but others saw the papacy of Gregory VII as the beginning of a period which reveals the inability of the movement to carry out the task it had set itself.

There are other factors which should be taken into account in our description of the period. The year 1054 saw the completion of what was known as "the great schism" between the Church in the East and the West, even though Islam was hampering the life of the Christian peoples in a thousand different ways. The same period also saw a process of great demographic expansion in the West, and the population increased from 46 million to 61 million between 1050 and 1200.[2] This growth in population was closely linked with the development of agriculture, the craft sector and industry, especially textiles.

All this caused an acceleration in the processes of social change. However, "Satisfied with the organized charity under its control, the Church took little interest in the processes undergone by the social conditions of peasants and craftsmen: it did not favour the *(cartas de franquía)* which could be obtained without resorting to violence, and it did not recognize in these collective movements any suitable application of its respect for spiritual values. Likewise, in the political sphere, it did not understand the extent of the communal movement, which many of its prelates saw as the result of revolutionary passions; most of the episcopates were indifferent or hostile to a trend inspired by the wish to put an end to the selfishness of the nobility. Consequently, at the same time as the Church continued to preach its gospel of justice and charity, its worldly commitment closed its eyes to necessary reforms."[3]

We know that there were at least three large groups or social classes in medieval society: the *oratores* (intellectuals, monks, clergy), the *bellatores* (nobles and soldiers), and *laboratores* (peasants, slaves, freemen, and so on). "This kind of structure not only offended against justice, but also placed great obstacles in the way of progress."[4] Some Christians were aware of this injustice, and were not blind to the alliance which often existed between *oratores* and *bellatores*. A large sector of the monastic movement also shared in this awareness, denouncing it as we have already mentioned briefly, and provoking the famous dispute over investitures. But what were the practical implications of this crisis ? To many historians,[5] all this is an indication of the serious upheaval that shook the Empire in this period of transition, which necessarily resolved itself in favour of the papacy, whose power would be taken as the expression of a form of theocracism. Unfortunately, the "Gregorian reform" failed to understand the communal movement, which in various ways rejected the feudal system and proposed not only institutional reform of the highest echelons of power but other deeper reforms of a structural nature. This reveals the limitations of the western monastic movement which, despite its influence within the Church, did not understand the need for social, economic and political reforms which could satisfy the hunger for justice of the expanding masses.

Social protest of the time, as was natural in that era, began to acquire a religious meaning. Thus, for example, the Catharist heresy captured the attention of the lower social sectors of Provence. Likewise, Joaquim of Fiore questioned the utopianism among the great Christian thinkers though without producing a break with the Augustinianism which dominated the theology of the time. But there were also much more radical attempts among the "working" sectors, especially the craftsmen in the textile and related industries.[6] In particular, we should mention the trend which started in Lyons around the movement begun by Peter Valdès; in Milan it took a different form, but it was also related to the Lyons movement; in Tuscany and Provence, it took the shape of the mendicant movements which had their models in Francis of Assisi and St Dominic Guzmán. All these movements can be seen as different expressions of protest against the prevailing social, economic and political order of the time.

Those movements, begun after the "Gregorian reform", such as the Franciscan movement, were basically a protest within the Church, but a protest nonetheless — against the limited extent of that reform. Almost all of them had two things in common: firstly, the requirement of poverty, not because they considered it an ideal, but because it was the means of sharing what many accumulated in abundance; and secondly, the freedom of mission, which was expressed in popular forms and through the values of popular culture. To put this in the words of Durand of Huesca, a follower of Peter Valdès who later returned to the official Church, it places the freedom to preach the

Christian message in close relationship with the problem of wealth, which *nolens volens* always supposes material concerns: "So that our spirit shall not be hindered by the love of riches, we propose, by the grace conferred upon us by God, to give our time to preaching and prayer, for according to the Lord's instruction, the workers are sent to reap; in other words, the preachers are sent to preach among the people. Thus, imitating the early Church, we dare to pledge ourselves to the task which the Lord entrusted to the 72." [7] It is a matter, then, of making the Church a body of the people, the Church of the people, and not of the gentry.

The Waldensian movement

As we mentioned above, Valdès' movement in Lyons was closely related to the movement of the "poor men of Lombardy" which certainly expressed at least part of the position of the communal movement in Northern Italy. The strength of the Lombardy communal movement can be appreciated when we remember that it defeated the army of the Emperor Frederick at the Battle of Legnano (1176). There is a difference of opinion concerning the origins of the Waldensian movement, but this is not what concerns us: we want here only to point out, in the words of Amedeo Molnar, that "The Waldensian movement is an evangelical form of Christian presence in the world, due either to the initiative of Valdès and his friends in Lyons and southern France, or to the initiative of the 'poor men of Lombardy'. The two initiatives can be considered as equal constituents of the movement" [8] According to Molnar, the Waldensians represent first of all a manifestation of the missionary and apostolic movement of the Church: they try to witness to Jesus Christ, to his righteous Lordship and life of love, *in the world*, and thus they break with the orientation of the western monastic movement in the Middle Ages. Secondly, the Waldensian movement included a social aspect, a class definition: they were not on the side of the rich, it was a movement of the poor, which exposed the responsibility of the rich and powerful for the social evils of the time. Third, and not least important, both elements unmistakably show that the Waldensian movement seeks to be part of the most radical evangelical tradition: the message of Jesus and some of the New Testament writings (the texts of Luke, the Epistle of James).

In the opinion of Molnar, who was a real authority on these "heretical" movements of the late Middle Ages, Peter Valdès (or the experience he symbolizes) represents on the one hand a clear realization of what it meant to be a disciple at that time, and on the other, closely linked with this, an unmistakable practice of Christian liberty. "The Christ of the Gospels met Valdès in a medieval city. He belonged to the new class which, thanks to the development of the cities, had acquired the liberty that gave freedom of movement to traders and craftsmen. The custom of making decisions with relative freedom also had its effect in the boldness with which he put into action the first consequences of their great meeting. For him, the return to the Gospel meant a break with the bonds of compromise. Persisting in poverty meant responding to Jesus' invitation to the style of life of a confessing believer in whom word and action formed an indivisible witness. It meant freeing the liberty of the Word of God from servitude to the feudal system of the Church: poverty should be the companion of missionary (i.e. itinerant) preaching. Suddenly, the position of Valdès and his friends was seen as a criticism of daily routine." [9]

As we can see, Valdès claimed to stand in the tradition of the mission given by Jesus to the Seventy (Luke 10). Poverty becomes a condition for liberty: only the poor, as Jesus was poor, are in a position to be free and to pledge their whole being to the mission entrusted to them by the Lord of the Gospel. They have no wealth to answer for, and therefore no ties which bind their action. This freedom is essential if the proclamation of the Gospel and the action it demands are not to be compromised by attachment to the powers of the world. Clearly, this position contains a radical criticism of the Constantinian synthesis and all that arose with it in the history of the Church, as we have seen in previous chapters.

But Valdès did not see the fulfilment of mission only as being able to preach the Word with freedom. It was much more than this. Mission leads to service to the poor, for this is the means of expressing the "*sequela Christi*", of being faithful to the Lord. "For the Waldensians, the Church of the hierarchy was still the Church of the Orthodox faith and the administration of the Sacraments, but there were defects in its preaching and practice of good works. So the Waldensians tried to correct these faults and set themselves to preach good works; that is, to the repentance and conversion necessary if they were to be carried out. Because of the avarice of the clergy and also of the faithful, Durand of Huesca understood 'good works' to mean service to the poor, the 'little brothers of Christ'. It is a direct call to *metanoia* which, towards the end of the 12th century, brought a revival of the kind of preaching typical of John the Baptist. But by so doing, the Waldensians invaded the field of action reserved to the hierarchy, and which it jealously guarded, and this caused the clergy to accuse them of *vituperatio* and *derogatio*; despite the intentions of their founder, this brought the Waldensian movement inexorably to the point of schism and heresy." [10] In all their efforts, they claimed to follow Christ, and to show that they were totally pledged to this "*sequela*".[11] Poverty seemed to them a testimony of submission to Christ, the way to be a disciple according to the Gospel, rather than an ideal to be pursued.

The relationship of the movement of the "poor men of Lyons" (in which religious and evangelical elements are undoubtedly clearer than social protests) with the "poor men of Lombardy" (among whom according to the information available the emphasis on social protest was predominant) gives a wider dimension to the Waldensian message. The "poor men of Lombardy" struggled to replace the feudal order by another, based on the existence of "*il comune*". This is the name given to the "group of poor men in the narrow sense, the preachers responsible for the two societies — the ultra-montane and the Italian. This use of language should not surprise the people of the time, who were familiar with the structure of political life. Indeed, the term *comune* referred to a voluntary, pledged association which constituted self-government (self-administration, we would say today) of the world of the city, and whose members ('the communists') together carried out certain functions and attributes previously the responsibility of the higher authority." [12]

Our knowledge of the events of the period suggests that this kind of protest, primarily expressed in religious terms but with a clear social and political content, was definitely "in the air" at this time. For example, there was another group connected with the Waldensians, the Humiliati, a community movement formed mainly by Italian textile workers. After belonging to the Waldensian movement, they later rejoined the Church of Rome, with their own rules. They believed that work was a means of attaining a worthy life; outside the set hours of work, their time was devoted to prayer and fasting. They lived in communities and sought perfect continence. While the "Humiliati" were accepted within the Church by Alexander III, the Waldensians were obliged to lead a clandestine life, particularly during the time of the Inquisition beginning in the 13th century.

The practice of faith in clandestinity did not mean a rejection of mission, that is, of witness to the Gospel, but in their clandestine life the believers had to have patience — to await the right moment to show themselves, the *kairos*, the appropriate time to witness. At the same time, they had to stand firm, for another characteristic of the Waldensian movement was a clear belief in the nearness of God's judgment: "The day of the Lord is at hand: do not waver in your faith." This was expressed in an eschatological hope, bringing with it hope in the justice of God which was to come about. Of course, none of this avoids the suffering of the poor, but it is a sign of faithfulness to the Lord, however hard the circumstances. The cross is not avoided; it is taken up. These movements were clearly evangelical in nature. The accusations of heresy made against them resulted from their clear message of social and religious protest. However, just as the Waldensians were accused of heresy, other similar movements (the " Humiliati ", for instance) were accepted within the Church — not, of course, without certain limitations. This acceptance was even more evident in the case of the Franciscans and Dominicans, the two Mendicant Orders founded early in the 13th century.

Why were some accepted while others were condemned? It would be unsafe to speculate. It seems, though, that by the beginning of the 13th century the authorities of the western Church (particularly Innocent III) must have become aware that the movements were powerful representatives of the hopes of the people from which the Church could not remain at a distance. All indications were that the church leaders thought that the "Gregorian reform" was succeeding, although its limitations were becoming evident. It was a reform of the institutions which wielded power, but not of the structures which arose from the exercise of power and through which society was organized. The Church realized that, in view of the problem posed by the existence of the poor, it was in danger of becoming isolated from the ordinary people. It must, therefore, open itself to the challenge. But how? — abstractly, or in a practical way? A practical response would have been to take the way in which the Waldensians posed the reform of missionary practice and fraternal service seriously. In other words, this would have led the Church to be concerned for the poor and their struggles. On the other hand, an abstract response would have meant giving first consideration to poverty itself, as an ideal.

The Mendicant Orders of the early 13th century

Unlike the Waldensian movement, the institutionalization of the Mendicant Orders gave them an official character, the stamp of orthodoxy, which the Waldensians did not have. There has been much discussion about the possible relationships between Waldensians and Franciscans [13] and between Waldensians and Dominicans. In the first case, there is an obvious convergence in that the poor were seen as privileged, and that both movements were clearly expressions of popular culture. In the second case, there was an evident affinity in missionary methods.[14] As we have already said, these points of convergence are part of the "atmosphere", the "spirit" of the age.

In the Franciscan movement, or more precisely in the life and thought of Francis of Assisi, there are two elements which bring the movement very close to the Waldensians. On the one hand, the rejection of the emerging structure of society expressed in the repudiation of the accumulation of wealth, which began to have an effect on commercial agreements and exchanges of the time. And on the other hand, just as the Waldensians attempted to bring democracy to the Christian community, the Franciscans in turn proposed the democratization of the cloisters, opening monastic life to the poor: "Hitherto, monks had belonged, as a rule, to the upper classes; only for the aristocrat was there open the refuge of the cloister. The poor, except in the towns, were serfs tied down to the soil; the heavenly walks were not for them, save possibly as lay brothers. But in the brotherhood of St Francis, caste distinctions were unknown: the men whom feudalism had despised took the world by storm. The very title of the Franciscan Order is almost untranslatable because of its democratic significance. In all the towns of Italy, the people were divided into 'majores' and 'minores'; the nearest equivalent would be 'guilded' and 'unguilded'. Francis deliberately changed the name of his disciples from the 'Penitents of Assisi' and enrolled himself with the unguilded; his was the company of the 'Brothers Minor'. The coming of the friars was one of the few great spiritual movements that have arisen directly from the people." [15]

This quotation from Workman answers the question with which we concluded our last point. St Francis did not respond to the challenge in the abstract, nor by withdrawing in "privacy", as some interpreters of his work would have us believe, but by "loving the poor and certainly not only from the mystic point of view".[16] In the Franciscan rule, as in the Dominican, poverty is one of the vows made on entry to the Order. But in both, as for Valdès, poverty is neither an ideal nor a virtue, but a condition for the itinerant ministry required by the fulfilment of the Church's mission. The message of Francis of Assisi also insists that it is through poverty that conditions are created which permit the renewal of the Church, releasing it from worldly powers and hence freeing it to struggle for love between human beings, without which true justice cannot exist. With this emphasis, the Church tended to leave behind the characteristics acquired during the period following the Constantinian synthesis, to become a free community in which equality and, therefore, democracy predominated among its members.

These movements, says A. Volpe, "represent something new, movements of a democratic character, directed towards aims which are both social and religious — religious explicitly and consciously, social only implicitly and uncertainly (for lack of social experience, and also because at that time even material need sought to find its satisfaction in a religious transformation)." [17] However, these words of Volpe reveal a difference between the "poor men of Lombardy" and the Mendicant Orders. As we can see, in the former, social concerns are conscious and are as important as religious matters, whereas they are not priorities for the Orders of St Francis and St Dominic. It should be clearly understood that this was the institutional expression, for, according to Alessandra Campagnano, St Francis at least not only loved "even the least of the disinherited", but also assumed the popular culture of his day and the social forms it implied. [18]

Unfortunately, the death of St Francis brought a resurgence of the Constantinian synthesis, although in new forms. St Dominic of Guzmán also had to overcome terrible opposition in order to include poverty in the vows for entry into the Order. In short, the new synthesis could be expressed as follows: the vow of poverty was required of the members of both Orders, but the Order itself could have possessions and wealth. In this sense, the synthesis expressed some of the limitations of the "Gregorian reform", which was not able to overcome the terms of the captivity of the Church at that time, a captivity to the structures of medieval power which prevented it from making a concrete response to the challenges of the poor — in other words, from responding in practical terms, and not merely in the abstract (for example, by a vow) to the challenge of poverty.

Lessons to be learned

This period was extremely important for the experience of the Church because it provided a series of lessons which are still valid for the Christian community today. We refer not so much to the situation as it began to take shape around the fourth decade of the 13th century, but rather to the dynamic experience of the Church between 1170 and 1230.

In the first place, the vocation of poverty arose as a means of following Christ, and can be understood in the framework of a *theologia crucis*. The vocation is a response not so much to the challenge of the poor but primarily to the call of the "poor man of God", Jesus Christ. This vocation to poverty does not make it an ideal for life, but an expression which indicates an attitude of openness to the demands of the Lord.

Secondly, since these demands have a missionary character ("Go and preach") the vocation of poverty is a condition for the freedom with which the Christian mission must be fulfilled. Openness presupposes that mission does not imply an attitude of triumphalism but, once again, a way of life under the cross: "For the Waldensian reform suffering has no value in itself; it is simply the possibility of authentic witness. The criterion by which this witness is to be judged is offered us by Jesus Christ himself, who came to his own but, far from being received, was put to death. We are witnessing to a *theologia crucis* applied to the historic existence of the Christian community." [19]

Taking up the cross, at least for the Waldensians, was expressed in two ways: first by a clandestine, missionary existence — terms which suggest a terrible tension, since mission cannot be hidden and, under the conditions we have described, it had to be carried out in secret. Second, they were always ready to go wherever necessary in order to witness to the Lord, to renew hope in his justice, and to help the poor. On the basis of their secrecy and the eager readiness to advance their work, it has been said that the Waldensians do not constitute part of the Church but rather a sect. Molnar's answer to this is: "But what is the relationship of the Church as a minority to the rest of society, and in what aspect is it universal? For the first Reform, there was a great temptation to withdraw to the level of a sect; the seduction of 'nicodemism' had to be resisted, and the second Reform rightly rebuked it. Moreover, *the first Reform discovered the new efficiency of the 'groups' ready to give witness in given situations*. The two simultaneous poles of its ecclesiology are *separation* and *missionary radiation*. On the one hand, then, the *discipline of secrecy* and on the other, the *itinerant ministry*." [20] In our view, both elements imply an affirmative response to the call of Jesus to take up the cross.

Thirdly, the practice of helping the poor, the criticism of riches and the willingness to accept poverty in accordance with the Gospel was an attitude which implied a protest against the ruling order. Among the Waldensians, it was "like a spiritual strike against prevailing economic forces",[21] while, for St Francis, it became a radical protest in the rejection of money, an attitude which, as we know, was later abandoned by the Order following the death of the *poveretto d'Assisi*. Now, if this is not understood simply in individual terms, that is, as being valid only for the believer, it acquires enormous importance for the life of the Church. Poverty then becomes a test which measures the Christian community's faithfulness to the mandate of the Gospel: "Sell all that you have, and give to the poor." Wycliffe also emphasized this line, pointing out that the Church abandoned this path when it allowed itself to become involved in the temptation of *temporali dominio*. Only a radical impoverishment could free it from this situation.[22]

This deepening by Wycliffe of the lines sketched by the Waldensians leads to our fourth comment: the element of radical criticism of society and the power structures of the Constantine order. According to the Czech thinker, Pierre Checicky, quoted by A. Molnar, *"The Church will be poor in the evangelical sense when it learns to renounce the class structure of society*. The power of coaction and violence cannot bring about among men the love of which Christ is the creator and living paradigm. According to Checicky, any faithful exegesis of the Sermon on the Mount must admit that the requirements formulated in it were not made to reassure the political order about its perfection." [23]

In other words, a practical response to the challenge of the poor leads to a position of militant and active criticism of unjust structures at the social and economic level, as well as of confrontation — in Gospel terms, this means a *theologia crucis* — with the power which maintains them. In those days it meant a confrontation with the Christian order in its medieval theocracy version which only sanctified "social injustices, the division of society into the classes of the clergy, the masters and the servants. *The Church of Christ must renounce*

*any type of accommodation with authoritarian power. It cannot become
the 'salt of the earth' unless it accepts the condition of a minority
community which presents to the world the true scandal of the cross."* [24]
This rejection of secular power and its unjust structures, although the
institutional Church may be participating in it, brings with it an
evangelical perspective of anxious expectation of the Kingdom of
God and his justice which will overthrow the wicked order of this
world once and for all.

Fifth, this hope, understood in active terms, must be expressed
in a way which corresponds to the culture and thinking of those who
have nothing to lose (because they possess nothing) and everything
to gain (because they hope for everything). In other words, one
lesson we can learn from the Waldensians, the poor men of Lombardy
and especially the Franciscans, is that practical solidarity with the
poor requires the formulation of a "popular pedagogy" which permits the masses to understand the meaning and urgency of the
Gospel message; and also a "popular theology" which reflects the
preoccupation of faith in the context of the thought, hopes and
struggles of the people. Both popular pedagogy and popular theology
— at least in the practice of the Waldensians and Franciscans —
meant a criticism of official teaching and doctrine.

We believe that both lines suggest very fertile possibilities for the
Church of today, especially if we bear in mind that pedagogy is not
so much the sophistication of the thought but rather the degree of
specificity with which the problems are posed. Moreover, we must
remember that in this theology the determining elements are those
which result from faithfulness to the Word of God in confronting
the established power (that is, its unjust structures) and in practising
assistance to the poor (those who struggle for *il comune*), accompanied by a life in community. So, the movements we have been
studying teach us that there is a way of doing theology and guiding
the people of God which corresponds to the life of the people and
which is different from the methods imposed by the dominant groups
for teaching and communicating the faith. The theological culture
of the Waldensians is a culture of the Word communicated by word
of mouth and as a community. In order to avoid persecution, this
communication had to be done in secret, but always keeping to the
Holy Scriptures as a norm for Christian witness.

Sixth — and the last point we shall mention — although this is
by no means exhaustive of the lessons we can learn from these move-

ments, all this implies living under the sign of the authority of Christ. In other words, the powers of this world are not accepted as definitive, but an attempt is made to see how, through the contradictions and developments of the ages, Christ opens the road which leads to the Kingdom of God. It would be a mistake to think that this road is a triumphal way. It is not the entry into Jerusalem on Palm Sunday, but the *via crucis* which leads to Golgotha. It therefore implies a tension between the triumphant coming of the Kingdom of God and the pain of knowing that, although everything seems ready for the Kingdom, the consequences of the sinful order which rules this world must still be suffered in militancy.

However, Christ dominates this world, crucified as King of Kings, risen but yet to appear in the fullness of his glory. Accepting the Lordship of Christ under these conditions means rejecting any claim to absolute rule over the life of men which so often characterizes earthly powers. So many times they omit to do what is necessary to advance justice among men, although they have the means in their hands. It is they who keep the poor in a situation of misery directly opposed to the will of God. In this case, the lesson of the poor Christians of the Middle Ages is that faith leads to militancy for justice against the powers which oppose the purposes of God. Today, as then, this generally implies taking up the cross. For the Lordship of Christ and his Kingdom are not obvious to all human beings, but are hidden to those who see with the eyes of this world. The *regnum Christi* does not yet imply the triumph of the Church, but *already* demands faithfulness to the radical instructions of the Lord.[25]

NOTES:

[1] In this regard, see DEMETRIOS J. CONSTANTELOS: *Byzantine Philanthropy and Social Welfare*. New Brunswick, New Jersey: Rutgers University Press, 1968.

[2] Figures given by Amedeo Molnar in: JEAN GONNET & AMEDEO MOLNAR: *Les Vaudois au Moyen Age*, vol. I, p. 18. Ed. Claudiana, 1974.

[3] M. D. CHENU: *L'Evangile dans le Temps*, p. 48. Paris, 1964.

[4] JEAN GONNET & AMEDEO MOLNAR: *Les Vaudois au Moyen Age*, Vol. I, p. 19, *op. cit.*

[5] Cf. RAFFAELLO MORGHEN, based on BARBAGALLO, CAGGESE & VOLPE: *Medioevo Cristiano*. Bari, 1951.

94   Good News to the Poor

[6] Apart from the book by Gonnet and Molnar quoted above, see ERNST TROELTSCH: *The Social Teaching of the Christian Churches*, Vol. I, p. 354. London: George Allen & Unwin; New York: Macmillan Co., third impression, 1950.

[7] DURAND of HUESCA: *Liber Antiheresis*, quoted by Gonnet and Molnar, pp. 61-62, *op. cit.*

[8] *Ibid.*, p. 1.

[9] *Ibid.*, p. 1.

[10] *Ibid.*, p. 63.

[11] Cf. AMEDEO MOLNAR: *La Protesta Valdese e la Prima Riforma*, when quoting Walter Map: "These people do not own houses. They travel in twos, barefoot, with no luggage, placing everything under common ownership following the example of the apostles. Naked, they follow the naked Christ." Ed. Quaderni di la Gioventù Italiana, 1966.

[12] *Ibid.*, p. 10.

[13] Cf. ERNST TROELTSCH: *The Social Teaching of the Christian Churches*, Vol. I, p. 355, *op. cit.*

[14] Cf. AMEDEO MOLNAR: *La Protesta Valdese e la Prima Riforma*, p. 7, *op. cit.*

[15] HERBERT B. WORKMAN: *The Evolution of the Monastic Ideal*, p. 297. London: Epworth Press, second edition, 1927.

[16] ALESSANDRA CAMPAGNANO: "La figura di Francesco di Assisi", in *Eretici e Ribelli del XIII et XIV Secolo*, p. 24. Libro a cura di Domenico Maselli, Pistoia: Ed. Zellini, 1974.

[17] A. VOLPE: *Eretici e Moti Eretici del XI al XV Secolo nei Loro Motivi e Riferimenti Sociali*, p. 26. Ed. Rinovamento, 1907.

[18] ALESSANDRA CAMPAGNANO: "La figura di Francesco di Assisi, p. 37 *op. cit.*

[19] JEAN GONNET & AMEDEO MOLNAR: *Les Vaudois au Moyen Age*, Vol. I, p. 428, *op. cit.*

[20] AMEDEO MOLNAR: *La Protesta Valdese e la Prima Riforma*, p. 39, *op. cit.*

[21] *Ibid.*, p. 5.

[22] JEAN GONNET & AMEDEO MOLNAR: *Les Vaudois au Moyen Age*, Vol. I, p. 423, *op. cit.*

[23] *Ibid.*, p. 424.

[24] AMEDEO MOLNAR: *La Protesta Valdese e la Prima Riforma*, p. 34, *op. cit.*

[25] See in this respect the excellent analysis by Mario Miegge of Calvin's exegesis of the parable of the talents (Matt. 25 : 14-30), in *I Talenti Messi a Profitto*, pp. 103 ff., especially pp. 105-109. Urbino: Ed. Argalia, 1969.

8 · Lessons for our Time

In the last chapter, we noted some lessons to be taken into account in our discussion of the problem of the challenge posed to the Church today by the poor and poverty.

1. The concept of poverty in the Scriptures is not limited solely to economic poverty. It refers rather to the dependent, the needy, whose life is limited, who therefore look to God to change their condition and bring justice. So poverty can never be considered a virtue; it is the result of evil, or, if you like, of the injustice which prevails in human relations. However, since the poor live in hope of justice, poverty becomes a condition for true piety — the quality of those who suffer but nevertheless continue to hope in the Lord and remain humble before God.

2. Jesus confirms this privilege of the poor, since He proclaims that they are to inherit the Kingdom. God, who undertakes to correct human mistakes, will give the keys of the Kingdom to the poor, for in the Kingdom justice will reign. It is natural that the victims of injustice and exploitation should be the first to receive the privilege of the Kingdom. Moreover, in Jesus we find a model of the way of life of the poor man who is also a "servant of Yahweh"; he is not resigned to his poverty, but practises the hope which kindles hope in others too.

3. All this implies a grave judgment on those who base their existence on the accumulation of wealth. Jesus' message to them is very clear: "God or Mammon. A man cannot serve two masters." Jesus calls the rich to renounce the goods of this world so that, through this act, they can prove that God — the God of justice and

love, who is the Lord — is in their hearts, but also so that they can show solidarity with those who suffer injustice and need caused by others' covetousness and love of riches. The rejection of the eagerness to accumulate wealth is one of the marks of the disciple of Jesus. The rich, more than any other social group, are the ones who must give up their wealth if they seriously desire to follow Jesus. This is why it is so difficult for a rich man to enter the Kingdom of God. The road to the Kingdom, at least for the rich, is signposted by the search for justice, in whose service they must offer their possessions as a sign of charity and solidarity with the less privileged, with those in the lowest rank of the social pyramid. This, too, was the road followed by God in Christ, who "though he was rich, yet for your sake became poor, so that by his poverty you might become rich" (II Cor. 8 : 9).

4. In the Christian communities of the first century after Christ, this understanding of the Gospel message concerning the poor and poverty was expressed in various ways which, though quite different, certainly had clear points of convergence. On the one hand, there was the community of goods, first practised among Christians in the Jerusalem community, but also found in other churches. Spiritual communion, the practice of the eucharist itself, was confirmed by this means of expressing basic solidarity among believers. Love between the faithful found concrete expression through the common ownership of possessions which, while not obligatory, was seen as a sign of the justice of the Kingdom so anxiously awaited by the first-generation Christians. On the other hand, in the thinking of St Paul as recorded in his Epistles, while the theme of poverty is not a priority, there was a clear indication that fraternal community requires active charity within the Church. Hence his eagerness to obtain funds for "the saints of Jerusalem". He urges the people to whom he writes to share with others, not by placing poverty in general on a pedestal of virtue, but offering as an example "the gift of Christ", who gave up his own divine condition to redeem humanity and the rest of creation.

However, it is in the Epistle of James that we find the most radical message (apart from Jesus') on the place which must be accorded to the poor in the Christian community and also on the Christian attitude towards the rich. For the author of this New Testament document, it is the rich who are "double-minded", that is, they live in a tension of indecision between following Jesus and loving wealth. This is the reason for his denunciation. On the other hand, James says that the poor are those who look for the Kingdom and its justice, and therefore they do not give their hearts to earthly things; they are in a better condition to practise true piety which cares for the lowliest (the "orphans and widows in their affliction, and to keep (themselves) unstained from the world" — James 1 : 27).

5. The records at our disposal show that these guidelines for the Christian attitude to the challenge of the poor and poverty became weaker as time passed, while certain inconsistencies began to appear in the way the Church dealt with the problem. However, at least in the early centuries of the Church's history, poverty was never considered a good thing, and still less a virtue, but the expression of evil. In the face of the resurgence of poverty at the beginning of the second century, the various Christian communities began to organize their assistance to the poor. A synthesis of positions then began to take shape: on the one hand the Church drew up guidelines for helping the poor, and their assistance was structured accordingly; on the other hand, certain bishops began to allow believers to adopt a more comfortable life style. So the problem of the poor was attacked only at the level of its consequences and not of its causes. The poor were still dependent on the rich and, although some of the rich showed great generosity, the institutional and structural injustice which generated poverty was not dealt with at its roots.

This synthesis of behaviour within the Church was an expression of the agreement reached at that time (third-fourth centuries) between Christian faith and classical culture, between the Church and the Empire, between Christian morality and dominant pagan customs. A radical reaction against synthesis came from the monastic movement, some of whose leading exponents (St Basil, St John Chrysostomos, etc.) harshly criticized the irresponsible economic growth which some people pursued at that time, neglecting the needs of their neighbours and especially the most humble of them. It was in this sense that St John Chrysostomos spoke of the "sacrament of brotherhood" which was to ratify the sacrament of the altar, the eucharist. Of course, this line of thinking was not new in the Church; St John had already mentioned it in his first epistle: "We know that we have passed out of death into life, because we love the brethren. He who does not love remains in death. Anyone who hates his brother is a murderer, and you know that no murderer has eternal life abiding in him. By this we know love, that He laid down his life for us; and we ought to lay down our lives for the brethren. But if anyone has the world's goods and sees his brother in need, yet closes his heart against him, how does God's love abide in him? Little children, let us not love in word or speech but in deed and in truth" (I John 3 : 14-18). For the exponents of the monastic movements, the existence of poverty runs parallel to the private and excessive accumulation of riches, which is considered to have its roots in injustice, since it is sinful, and in the misuse of wealth.

6. It is the duty of the rich to show solidarity with the poor. The thirst for riches is incompatible with the Gospel, which emphasizes the practice of neighbourly love, particularly for the meekest of our neighbours. Service to the poor is a precious opportunity of witnessing to our discipleship of Jesus. However, in spite of its insistence, the monastic movement did not manage to get its opinions and interpretations of the Gospel accepted by the majority of church members. The Church's response was to organize its service to the poor in such a way as to alleviate the suffering of the victims of injustice, but not to attack its causes. In both East and West, this led to the establishment of orphanages, hospitals and homes which encouraged many who had possessions to become private benefactors. For its part, the imperial power, particularly Byzantium, defined philanthropy as a virtue to be practised.[1]

7. When far-reaching socio-economic changes began to take place in the 12th-13th centuries, especially in western Europe, the economic situation obviously affected the population which had almost doubled within a period of one century. The more alert Christians could not ignore the challenge of the poor, and the Church's mission thus came to be understood as being closely connected with the serfs, the peasants, the dispossessed. The popular movements of those days in the West expressed their protests in terms which were clearly Christian, and the projects they envisaged implied the reform not only of society but of the Church itself. Peter Valdès and the poor men of Lyons, together with the poor men of Lombardy, are unmistakable witnesses to this movement, as were the Franciscans and Dominicans. In other words, the positive response to the challenge of the poor led to the emergence in one sector of the western

Church of those days of a current of social transformation which sought to attack the problem of poverty at its very roots, that is, by struggling against the injustice which produced it. Various forms of struggle were attempted: confrontation with the established power (the new form of the *Corpus Christianum* resulting from the "Gregorian reform" of the monk, Hildebrand, who became Pope under the name of Gregory VII); practical solidarity with the dispossessed through charity and, within limits, the community of goods; and the postulation of a form of social organization based on the sovereignty of the people *(il comune)*.

Theologically, in the final instance, these movements were faithful to the Word of God, as it was understood by the community of believers, rather than as a dogma defined and imposed by the powerful. This faithfulness to the Word — at least for the Waldensians — was expressed in a life of poverty (their way of witnessing to their anxious expectation of the Kingdom) and in the practice of forms of community life. As we know, the official position of the Church concerning these movements was not unanimous; while it persecuted the Waldensians and the poor men of Lombardy, it accepted within it the "Humiliati" (an offshoot of the Waldensians), those who lived under the rule of St Francis, and also the followers of St Dominic.

However, there is one point worth emphasizing here: the Waldensians and other similar movements were concerned not so much with *poverty* as with the existence of the *poor* and their problems. The same might be said of St Francis. On the other hand, there are those who point out that, for other movements of the late Middle Ages, the main concern was of a mystical and theoretical order (adherence to poverty, vows of poverty, marriage with "Dame Poverty"), rather than a concrete one. Hence many of them were faced with the tension between personal commitment to poverty, taking vows of poverty, while the institution to which they belonged continued to accumulate wealth and power. Could there be any escape from this situation? This is an issue which the churches still have to resolve.

The challenge of the poor and poverty to the churches today

We do not intend to make a systematic or detailed analysis of how the churches treated the problem in the period from the 14th century to the present day. A separate volume will deal with how the problem was posed in the process of social change which came with the industrial revolution in the West, and another volume will discuss in detail how the problem is posed in our time, the way the churches are responding to it, and what opportunities their response suggests for the renewal of the life of church institutions. Here we shall see what conclusions can be drawn for the life of the Church today from the past which we have been discussing. But before we do this, we must remember that the problem of the poor and poverty is posed quite differently today compared with the times we have reviewed in these pages. On the one hand, the number of poor people in the world has reached a level which no one could have foreseen so very long ago. And on the other, in qualitative terms, each day takes the poor further and further away from the possibility of breaking out of their bonds. They are incapable of overcoming them; the structures of injustice and oppression which generate their poverty seem to condemn them to a constant deterioration in their condition.[2]

Faced with these facts, our societies seem unable to join forces and struggle against the scourge of poverty, to destroy these structures of injustice and oppression which produce and nourish poverty, to see that the tremendous technological progress of our time is placed at the service of the less favoured and not the most powerful, to put a stop once and for all to the fearful arms race to which the world's powerful have committed themselves and to use this capital to struggle against the injustice, hunger, illiteracy, sickness and misery which afflict millions upon millions of our neighbours. Christians cannot ignore the facts. As Philip Potter, general secretary of the World Council of Churches, said in his message to the United Nations World Food Conference, Christians are motivated to respond to this challenge by their belief in a God of justice and love: "This concern of the churches is no new thing. Christianity has its origins in the Hebrew prophetic cry for justice and a shared community of all human beings made in the image of God. Above all, its name derives from the One who came proclaiming the Kingdom of God and his justice, and expressed this message in very concrete words and acts on behalf of the hungry, the thirsty, the naked, the oppressed, the outcasts of society. Indeed, He demonstrated his identification with them when He encouraged his followers to continue his attitude and action with the words: 'As you do it to the least of these my brethren, you have done it to me.' Throughout these nearly two thousand years, Christians have sought to serve all those who are in distress of any kind, and to help them to have a more humane existence through hospitals, schools, agricultural projects, and the teaching of skills of various kinds. In fact, the foundations of the economic and social affluence of the rich countries today were laid by the intrepid and sacrificial efforts of Christian monks, Orders, societies, etc. In the past two hundred years of western colonial and economic exploitation of the poor, underdeveloped countries — thanks to superior technology and arms — it was the churches which in large measure attempted to attend to the needs of the poor and oppressed, particularly through the work of missions and agencies of social service." [3]

In view of the situation we have described, Christians who are motivated in the way Philip Potter suggests have no choice but to face this crisis. Today the problem of the challenge posed by the poor cannot be faced solely by alleviating the consequences of poverty. The matter is so vast that, while we must organize ourselves to help the victims of hunger, sickness, oppression and injustice, we must also attack the causes of the evil. This implies the attempt to transform the structures which institutionalize oppression at the world level instead of helping to extend justice. We must not forget that, for the Christian, poverty and the existence of the poor in this world are a scandal, which is why the Kingdom is promised to them, to change their condition.

Unfortunately, although Christ's words on the subject are as clear as daylight, Christians are still divided in their response to the challenge of the poor in our time. Perhaps this is because the term "poverty" can be misunderstood. But even if this word is ambiguous (there is after all "spiritual poverty", "moral poverty", "material poverty", "intellectual poverty" and so on, often differing greatly from each other), the condition of being poor — physically poor — is unequivocal. Faced with someone who is poor, we either show solidarity or rejection (since indifference is the same as rejection). According to Gustavo Gutierrez: "The term *poverty* designates in the first place *material poverty*, that is, the lack of economic goods necessary for a human life worthy of the name. Christians, however, often have a tendency to give material poverty a positive value, considering it almost a human and religious ideal. It is seen as austerity and indifference to the things of this world and a precondition for a life in conformity with the Gospel. The double and contradictory meaning of *poverty* implied here gives rise to the imposition of one language on another and is a frequent source of ambiguities. The matter becomes even more complex if we take into consideration that the concept of material poverty is in constant evolution. On the other hand, poverty has often been thought of and experienced by Christians as part of the condition — seen with a certain fatalism — of marginated peoples, the 'poor', who are an object of our mercy. What we mean by material poverty is a subhuman situation. The Bible also considers it this way. Concretely, to be poor means to die of hunger, to be illiterate, to be exploited by others, not to know that you are being exploited, not to know that your are a person. It is in relation to this poverty — material and cultural, collective and militant — that evangelical poverty will have to define itself." [4]

When, instead of talking about "poverty", we try to understand the problem starting from the actual situation of the poor, then we can see that this is an expression of human sin, because it "represents a sundering both of solidarity and also of communion with God. Poverty is an expression of a sin, that is, of a negation of love. It is therefore incompatible with the coming of the Kingdom of God, a Kingdom of love and justice. Poverty is an evil, a scandalous condition, which in our times has taken on enormous proportions. To eliminate it is to bring closer the moment of seeing God face to face, in union with other men." [5]

To eradicate poverty is to end the situation in which anyone is poor. Is this a utopian dream? Yes, if we want all poor people to overcome their poverty from one day to the next. But not if the change is seen as the result of a continuous struggle for justice, for equality, for the wellbeing of all, which necessarily demands a sustained effort over several generations. What matters is this effort of solidarity, this practice of costly hope, which brings good news for the future. By making a decision of this kind, we can live in solidarity, struggling for a new lifestyle, which then gives rise to the emergence of "new ways of living poverty which are different from the classic 'renunciation of the goods of this world'. " [6]

Interpretations for our time of crisis

Why should ours be considered a "time of crisis" ? Not, we believe, because of the effects of the higher prices of raw materials, nor the monetary instability which goes with it, nor growing unemployment, but mainly because never before the present decade has there been such a wide gap — indeed, a contradiction — between the rich minorities of our planet and the masses who are struggling for survival. It is a mistake to think there is no connection between the two; it takes little effort to see that the affluence of the few is nurtured to a great extent by the misery of the many. The contradictions and tensions which this produces between the two sides can reach the danger point, and this is why it is time to retrace our steps and take a straighter path. Unless we do, the consequences for future generations may be incalculably serious. But the problem affects not only those yet unborn; the situation *today* is already so grave that we cannot delay. But what can we do?

First of all, the rules which define economic growth must be changed. We have been working for vast growth, without realizing what kind of growth we are achieving. It has been and still is a type of growth which has institutionalized injustice, because for a small portion of the population of the world (only about 20 %), it has produced a situation of wellbeing unimaginable hardly a generation ago, while the rest seem condemned to struggle for survival in misery, which is the same as dying without hope. It is a kind of economic growth for the sake of which we have not hesitated to invest vast sums in the development of the "industrial/military complex", a veritable death machine, which basically helps the powerful who can consolidate their privileged situation. It is a kind of growth which excludes the majority and offers them no possibility of a share in it.

This reminds us of some of St Ambrose's words to the rich, whose responsibility in this field is so serious: "Do you hear, rich man, what the Lord says? You come to the church not to distribute anything to the poor but to take something away from them; you fast, not so that the cost of your meal may benefit the poor, but in order to seize all that he has. What pretence are you making with the book, the letters, the seal, the notes, the link with the law? Have you not heard? 'Break all the fetters of injustice, unfasten the bonds that oppress, let the oppressed go free, and break the evil yoke.' You offer me the tablets on which the law is inscribed, but I propose to you the law of God; you write with ink, but I repeat to you the oracles of the prophets, written under the inspiration of God; you prepare false witness, I ask for the witness of conscience, from whose judgment you can neither escape nor free yourself, whose witness you cannot refute in the day when God reveals the hidden works of men. You say: 'I will pull down my barns' (Luke 12 : 18); but God says: 'Rather give up what is enclosed in your barns, give it to the poor, so that the needy may make use of these resources.' You say: 'I will make them bigger, and use them to store my harvests, however abundant they are.' But the Lord says to you: 'Share your bread with the hungry.' You say: 'I will take the poor men's houses from them.' But the Lord says to you: 'Welcome to your house the needy who have no roof over their heads.' Rich man, why do you think God will listen to you if you do not think you need to listen to God?" [7]

If we try to express this in words which are more in keeping with present thinking, we might say that growth must be decided according to a responsible social criterion and not just the interests of private gain. In this context, there is need for reflection, not so much on the "limits to growth" as the Club of Rome has attempted,[8] but on what type of growth we should seek. The present lines of economic growth consolidate existing inequalities: isn't it time we sought more harmonious and less dependent growth? The application of social criteria implies an attempt at development which emphasizes quality rather than quantity (which does not mean that quantity is irrelevant), and this must take the shape of priorities which express a social criterion rather than goals that continue to permit individual accumulation which always benefits the "biggest fish".[9] The search for development which gives priority to social and collective aspects means upsetting this order of things and correcting our mistakes.

Secondly, our societies must aim for the greatest possible justice. The Second General Assembly of the Latin American Episcopate in Medellín, September 1968, said: "Justice is the new name for peace." Indeed, without equality between the different sectors of society, social tensions cannot be overcome; antagonisms and contradictions tend to become more acute. Justice becomes a condition for peace, and when the distance between social groups tends to diminish, the possibilities of confrontation and conflict also decrease. Here, we should recall what St Augustine says in his *Commentary on the Psalms* concerning Psalm 85: "Mercy and truth came together; justice and peace embraced each other. Do justice and you will have peace, so that justice and peace may embrace. If you do not love justice you will not have peace, for the two love and embrace each other. He who does justice finds peace; peace embraces justice. They are friends. Perhaps you love one and not the other, for there is no one who does not love peace, but not everyone wants to act justly. If you ask all men, 'Do you love peace?' all the human race answers together, 'I love it, I desire it, I long for it.' Therefore, they must love justice, for they are friends and embrace each other If you do not love the friend of peace, it will not love you and will not come to you. Do you think it is a great thing to desire peace? Any perverse man desires it. Well, it is a good thing, peace. But do justice, for justice and peace embrace each other and do not fight." [10]

The simplicity of the writing of the bishop of Hippo does not disguise the depth of his thought. Especially in our time, when peace is preserved by a balance of terror and symmetries of armed power, we must remember that this is an illusion while there is so little justice among the peoples. The superpowers maintain this kind of armed peace between them, but meanwhile the people outside are torn apart by wars. And when we look at the basic causes of these confrontations, we see that there has always existed — at least in one of the parties to the conflict — the desire for greater equity in society. Isn't it time we learned, once and for all, that social justice cannot be ignored, and that we must strive for justice at the same time as we strive for peace?

Thirdly, and especially important for those who believe in Jesus Christ, another of the lessons of the past in our subject is that the accumulation of riches discredits the testimony of the Gospel. This is a lesson which seems to have been forgotten rather frequently by the world's Christian peoples, who are generally the richest. On many occasions, the witness of action has cast doubt on the witness of the Word. "How can we consider it anything but the height of folly to store everything in a place where it will be spoiled and ruined, and not leave the least bit where it will remain intact and even grow? And it is there that we are to live for all eternity! This is why the Gentiles do not believe what we say. They want us to show them a doctrine not through our words but through our works. But when they see us building magnificent houses, planting gardens, building baths, buying fields, they find it hard to believe that we are preparing a journey to another city. If this were true, they say, they would sell all that they own and deposit it there in advance, and this is how they see what often happens in life." [11]

Compared with this, the witness of people like Mother Teresa in the slums of Calcutta, or Dom Helder Camara in Recife, or Manas Buthelezi in South Africa, is more powerful than any kind of writing or preaching. With such people we cannot distinguish between social action and witness, for it is their social action which reveals the authenticity of their faithful witness to Jesus Christ.

Fourthly, we must insist that we should avoid the offer, often found in the past, of a solution of synthesis to the challenge posed to the Church by the poor, but which in the end does not help to present a clear response to it. By this, we mean that "dual" solutions are unsatisfactory to the Christian spirit. We cannot remain untroubled if some take a decision which commits them completely while others still swim between two currents. In other words, the Christian conscience cannot be satisfied because some pledge their whole being to the fight against injustice and solidarity with the poor, while others, generally the great majority, continue to live in complicity with the system of oppression which the former combat. For instance, as the Waldensian movement developed, the requirement of poverty and itinerant ministry which Valdès had put to the members of the movement remained valid only for some. On this point, Amedeo Molnar says: "It is not a matter of reducing the programme of poor and itinerant preaching to a piece of advice valid only for the elites; this was exactly the contrary of what Valdès had expected." [12] Precisely, in our time it is a matter of seeing if *all* the churches and *all* Christians, given the gravity of the problem of the poor today, cannot try to formulate a consistent and unbroken line of action in their efforts to combat poverty, which is equivalent to saying combating injustice, oppression and inequality.

Signposts to be followed
On the basis of what we have said, we should like now to offer some guidelines for the organization of our action as Christians in response to the challenge of the poor today.

I. Their situation demands our fundamental solidarity. "Only authentic solidarity with the poor and a real protest against poverty as it appears today can give a concrete and vital content to a theological speech on poverty. The lack of a sufficient commitment to the poor, the excluded and exploited, is perhaps the basic cause of the lack of solid and up-to-date thinking on the witness of poverty." [13] Fundamental solidarity with the poor means not only being open to them but accompanying them in their struggles against the injustices which they suffer and those who generate them. It also means, where indicated, that we must cease our solidarity with those who often oppress the poor and denounce their injustice.

II. We must recognize the demonstrated dynamism of the poor in the process of history. True, it cannot be denied that the awareness of the poor of the need to struggle against injustice and the other causes of poverty did not arise spontaneously, but was encouraged by the tenacious, dedicated and persistent work of people who, although not originally poor, have decided to join forces with the poor to fight against oppression and social inequality. But by doing so, they affirmed that the elites on their own can never achieve much, and that it is always the masses which in the final instance can change history.[14] This implies that the struggle against poverty not only requires the social force of the poor, but also demands that they be allowed to express themselves and to take the meaning and direction of their struggles into their own hands. Consequently, paternalism — wherever it occurs, whether implicit or explicit — must be constantly recognized and rejected by those who seek to express their solidarity.

III. In the development of these forces, those who believe in Jesus Christ must maintain an attitude of hope, for in the last instance their gaze is fixed not only on the process of social change which must be carried out, but, above all, on the Kingdom which the poor are to inherit. In other words, Christian participation in the struggle against injustice must not be hidden participation, but open. The Gospel is the salt of the earth and the light of the world, and those whose action is motivated by it, in the hope of the Kingdom it proclaims, must not hide themselves nor remain in the shadow. Only thus can any attempt to reduce the strength of the Gospel words and to seek compromises with the ruling order be corrected. "The Gospel is rich in social morality, in equalitarianism and revolutionary ethics. It is amazing with what obtuseness scholars and preachers move unheeding through its pages, or, with heavy insensitiveness, busy themselves with taking the edge off the Sermon on the Mount. Historically, it was regarded by the authorities as of real danger, because it was preached as the authoritative Word of God, enunciated by an accredited messenger sent to herald the actual and the immediate end of the existing order. It is the Messianic hope which like tinder awaited the spark, the Messianic framework of the whole life and teaching of Jesus, that gave point and force to what might so easily have been mere moral talk or harmless idealism." [15]

IV. This assumes the development of militant faith, which not only lives in the hope of the Kingdom, ready to collaborate with anyone who might even unconsciously be an agent of the will of God which works through history, but is also expressed through actions which testify that love is the dynamic factor which opens up the paths of justice. But now love's priority is those who are generally excluded from the life of society, those who are subdued and forgotten by the sectors which plan and programme the future. Living in the practice of love means adopting a theological perspective which, while not forgetting the resurrection, understands that human life must pass *via* the cross. Only thus, without triumphalism, and recognizing that we cannot avoid either suffering or pain, can we confront the powers of this world, the true counterpowers of Jesus Christ. Only thus, at moments when the "principalities and powers of the air" violate the rights of the poor, subject them to silence and refuse to let them express themselves, limiting them more and more to the confines of their poverty, is it possible for the believer to confront them. Not because he will vanquish them through his own strength; the victory is not his, but Christ's. But the road He treads to overcome the chains which bind our fellow men is not our road. His path is not the "archway of triumph" but the way of the cross. This does not mean we should preach resignation but rather the militancy which cannot avoid suffering, continual correction, the often costly but always generous practice of love, and solidarity with the poorest to whom Christ promised his everlasting presence.

V. As a consequence of this, we must take care not to risk compromises which jeopardize the witness of faith. Here we should recall once again the words with which John Lewis concludes his book, quoted above: "We cannot expect any recovery of the Jesus of history in those who are reconciled to the social order and its moral values, or who flinch from class and party strife. The apocalyptic crisis has descended upon our age, not prematurely as in the time of Jesus, but in the fullness of time. Opportunity as it confronts us is also the final sifting of chaff from wheat, the day of judgment. The Church may try, but it cannot succeed today in crucifying the Christ. The new Christ should be like an insurgent Proletariat, the uprisen people of God, and the Church which fails to do him reverence must be cast forth into the outer darkness. The Day of the Lord is at hand." [16]

May God grant that, until that day comes, we may serve the poor in their struggle, accompanying them in their journey towards a better world, showing solidarity with them as a testimony of the love and faithfulness due to Christ, as if we had found among them the crucified and risen Lord, ready to intervene with the justice of his Kingdom and thus overcome our world and its evil structures which abuse the least privileged of its people.

NOTES:

1 DEMETRIOS J. CONSTANTELOS: *Byzantine Philanthropy and Social Welfare*, pp. 43-65. New Brunswick, New Jersey: Rutgers University Press, 1968.

2 Cf. "Threats to Survival" — Document approved by the Central Committee of the World Council of Churches, August 1974, Berlin, in *Study Encounter*, Vol. X, No. 4, 1974, pp. 1-2.

3 Speech given by Dr Philip Potter at the United Nations World Food Conference, Rome, 11 November, 1974.

4 GUSTAVO GUTIERREZ: *A Theology of Liberation*, pp. 288-289. London, SCM Press, 1974.

5 *Ibid.*, pp. 295-296.

6 *Ibid.*, p. 301.

7 St AMBROSE: *Libro sobre Nabot de Yizreel*, MPL, T. XVII, Col. 780.

8 DONELLA H. MEADOWS, DENNIS L. MEADOWS, JØRGEN RANDERS, WILLIAM H. BEHRENS: *The Limits to Growth*. New York: Signet, 1972.

9 Cf. CHARLES ELLIOTT & FRANÇOISE DE MORSIER: *Patterns of Poverty in the Third World*, pp. 4-14. New York: Praeger, 1975.

10 St AUGUSTINE: *Comentario sobre los Salmos*, MPL, T. XXVII, Col. 1078.

11 St JOHN CHRYSOSTOMOS: *Homilia sobre San Mateo*, MPG, T. LVI, Col. 697.

12 AMEDEO MOLNAR: *La Protesta Valdese e la Prima Riforma*, p. 40 ff., *op. cit.*

13 GUSTAVO GUTIERREZ: p. 372, *op. cit.*

14 Toward the end of the classical age, St Augustine had reached conclusions of this same type. Cf. *La Ciudad de Dios*, MPL, T. XLI, Col. 464.

15 JOHN LEWIS: *Christianity and the Social Revolution*, p. 92. London: Victor Gollancz, 1935.

16 *Ibid.*, p. 102.

APPENDIX

CCPD and its Present Definition for Participation in the Struggle of the Poor and the Oppressed

At the Fifth Assembly of the WCC, it was proposed within the framework of the hearing on "Justice and Development" and later on accepted by the plenary of the Assembly, that CCPD should focus its action for the coming period on participation and support in the struggle of the poor and oppressed for more just and participatory societies. However, such a definition is not totally new to CCPD. As a matter of fact, it reflects a process which took several years but which was gradually and logically followed since the Ecumenical Consultation on Development Projects (Montreux 1970) till Nairobi. In what follows, there is an attempt to show how that process took place, but also to answer some questions about where we are, with whom we are going to work and for what, what is the theological awareness of our work, etc.

I. The line that led CCPD to the affirmation that development is the result of the struggle of the poor and the oppressed

1. The initial step was the definition of development as an inter-related process of economic growth, self-reliance and social justice (Montreux, 1970). That view of development was understood as a tool in the struggle against poverty, underlined by the search for social justice, while self-reliance indicates that there is the need to overcome situations of dependency. At the CCPD Commission Meeting in Driebergen (July 1972), the convergence of this line with that of the struggle for liberation that the poor and oppressed develop in many ways and in different contexts was pointed out.

2. The decision by CCPD to work with national counterparts illuminated some important implications of the struggle for development. The CCPD Network Meeting held at Bossey (April 1973; cf. *CCPD Dossier on "People's Participation in Development"*) indicated that:

"In many places all over the world people are becoming aware that development is more than the application of economic models to move a society from backwardness to modernization. Too many of the so-called developing countries are facing the results of a solely growth-oriented development which was devised by mostly western-educated planners, executed at great social costs and which, because of its reliance on external resources, has strengthened structures of domination and dependence. ...Development (seems to be) the game of the few who have access to knowledge, resources and power. A great part of the population of many developing countries is not involved in the development process other than in a passive way; it does not share the profits accruing from it, and is often affected only in a negative sense. And yet, people are getting ready to work towards participation in their own development." (*Op. cit.*, pp. 1-2).

The quotation seems important because it shows that the struggle of the poor is not only *against* their condition, namely poverty, but also *for* a new society, which is envisaged as an open one *for* people's participation, and hence opposed to marginalization.

3. The results of the Bossey CCPD Network meeting provided CCPD with valuable material for reflection. The findings of it were reflected in the CCPD Commission Meeting held at Albano, Italy (June 1973), and they indicate how CCPD was progressing in that direction:

"What we have learned is that there is another *programme style, based on people's participation and organization, by which their* poor become agents of their own development, identifying their needs, mobilizing their resources, shaping their future, and in which input resources from beyond is the complementary enabler." (*First Few Lessons*, a preparatory paper for the CCPD Commission Meeting at Albano, June 1973, pp. 2-3).

4. In the same paper, it was stated that:

"We are learning also that the starting point (of CCPD work) *is among the poor and the oppressed*, among peasants and industrial workers. They are the beneficiaries of their own action. The struggle is essentially theirs, and the decisions as to the nature of the struggle and its course is theirs also." (*First Few Lessons*, p. 3).

Following that line, in another preparatory paper for the same meeting it was said that:

"CCPD conceives development as a process through which people participate directly in their own liberation. In this way, development is the action that people themselves take to change their situation, rather than the result of an increase in the goods and services available to them. Therefore CCPD underlines the fundamental importance of people's participation in a true development process." (*Strategy Paper*, p. 1. CCPD Commission Meeting at Albano, Italy, June 1973).

The struggle for participation and liberation implies the search for a new society which, although it cannot be confused with the Kingdom of God, is clearly more indicative of it than societies in which domination and people's marginalization predominate.

5. The study sponsored by CCPD on *Poverty 2000* has led us to conclude that eradication of poverty can be achieved through deep transformation of a system in which "the poor subsidize the rich", and which gives to the rich privileges which are consolidated by social structures. (Cf. C. Elliott and F. De Morsier: *Patterns of Poverty in the Third World*, New York: Praeger Publishers, 1975. pp. 1-2. Cf. also pp. 350-355). Such transformation of prevailing systems should touch not only economic, social and political structures, but also cultural ones, on which the technological influence is so clear to create conditions which do not enable the poor and oppressed to become self-reliant:

"But perhaps more fundamental than anything else is the rupture of the dependence upon international standards and international approval of local technical developments. In many fields, from education to water supply, from industrial technology to social welfare, we have seen how, even in countries that have been relatively successful in breaking many patterns inherited from the colonial past, technological dependence remains unchallenged." (*Patterns of Poverty in the Third World*, p. 396, *op. cit.*)

6. Richard N. Dickinson, in the last chapter of his book about ecumenical involvement for justice and liberation in the period between the Uppsala and Nairobi Assemblies of the WCC, indicates that one of the clearest priorities for further work is to be *centred on the poorest:*

"Why should churches focus on the marginated? Certainly, that is the incontrovertible testimony of the Judeo-Christian heritage. At heart, the churches have the moral imperative to help those in distress — to feed the hungry, clothe the naked and visit the sick simply because they are in need. Another reason (not necessarily deeper or better) for the churches' primary action among the poor is that such action can contribute to the liberation of the rich, just as God has used the simple to confound the wise. It is often through the poor that we can demythologize the pretension and values used by those in power which frustrate the creation of a new age. Concentration on the poor, then, is not only a response to moral demands for justice and human dignity, it is also a way to freeing the affluent." (R. N. Dickinson: *To Set at Liberty the Oppressed*, pp. 116-117. Geneva: World Council of Churches, 1975.)

7. In a workshop organized in the framework of the CCPD Study on "Domination and Dependence", there was emphasized the need to promote international relations of the organized poor and oppressed with a view to confronting national and international injustices and dominations:

"The need for an organized resistance movement of the oppressed which would express itself in words and deeds, denouncing and combating the structures of domination and destroying the machinery of injustice throughout the world. Confronted with the spectre of the powerful and omnipresent multinational corporations, the creation of an "international movement of the poor" must receive the highest priority. And the churches, which in varying degrees have shared in oppression, must support the cause of the poor throughout the whole world by committing themselves resolutely to opposing the systems of domination and exploitation." (*To Break the Chains of Oppression*, p. 48. Geneva: World Council of Churches, 1975.)

8. At the Nairobi Assembly, this process was confirmed and encouraged. The churches, through their participation in develop-

ment, are discovering not only the validity of the promise of Jesus to the poor that they will inherit the Kingdom, but also that social sciences and history indicate humanization and liberation. It was stated there:

> "The development process should be understood as a liberating process aimed at justice, self-reliance and economic growth. It is essentially a people's struggle in which the poor and the oppressed are and should be the active agents and immediate beneficiaries.
>
> Seen in this perspective, the role of the churches and the WCC is to support the struggle of the poor and the oppressed towards justice and self-reliance.
>
> Three main programme areas are indicated for such work of the WCC:
>
> — Establish contacts for support with organizations of the poor and people's movements. International network.
>
> — Take experimental initiative to assist a few poor congregations to become the church of the poor and the oppressed, struggling against their own poverty and oppression. The importance of theological reflection in this context is underlined.
>
> — Struggle for change of oppressive structures at all levels.
>
> The concern for a new international economic order requires action, study and the improvement of new lifestyles." (WCC: Fifth Assembly, Nairobi, December 1975. Sub-hearing on "Justice and Development").

II. With whom and for what are we going to participate?
The struggle of the poor and the oppressed

The decision taken at Nairobi pushes CCPD into the struggles of our times. But it is clear that we are not discovering the reality of social, economic and political combats in which are involved the peoples, races, classes and ideologies of the present world. We are only going to have a more frank participation, making a clear option in favour of the oppressed and the poor. However, because the struggles have been going on, it is appropriate to look at their history in order to understand how they have evolved, trying to learn from them for the sake of our orientation. This is the maximum required if we want to play a responsible role in the exercise of our participation.

In a very synthetic way, the history of social struggles during the last 100 years shows us:

a) That there are *struggles of resistance*, promoted by spontaneous reaction of the people vis-à-vis burning issues (hunger, unbearable situations, etc.). They are indications both of injustices and of people's potential for change for a more just situation. However, it must be pointed out that these *struggles of resistance* are limited and do not endure for a long time; as soon as they have achieved some of their goals, the struggle generally comes to an end. Because of this fact, there is the impression that it is not difficult for the forces confronted by the resistants to cope with this kind of movement (at least partially). We can say that these struggles are limited both in vision and in time.

b) There are also *struggles for change*. They are motivated not only by reactions and resistance against injustice and oppression, but mainly by a deliberate plan for the achievement of a better society. In these cases, the point of the vision of a new society is fundamental. Up to 25 years ago, such visions were nourished by classical socialist values. Although they continue to be necessary ingredients for the vision of a better society, more and more those who strive for the accomplishment of it are underlining the importance of participatory structures and the building up of "people's power" at local, regional, international and national levels.

A major characteristic of the movements, groups and parties involved in this kind of struggle is that they do not understand themselves as an end *per se*, but as tools of the people in their efforts for change, and especially of the poor. Another element which characterizes them is that their organization generally is established in function of the goals that they want to achieve. In this sense, their organization is also some kind of indication of the type of society. which they are striving for. A third characteristic is that their *understanding* of reality is based on an appraisal of its dynamic and contradictory nature. This implies that, when these *movements* come into action, they progress through confrontation with their opponents, but always *for* a more equitable society.

c) An important point to be noted here is that in most of the cases the *movements for change* (not so much the *movements of resistance*) are the result of the action of activists:

> "The struggle for justice is essentially the struggle of the people themselves. However, the question has often been raised whether the people take up struggle by themselves, or whether it is precipitated by a catalyst, "the agents of change". The question in itself may be irrelevant in the final analysis. In the historical perspective, it can be said that all popular movements of any significance resulted not from a spontaneous act of binding together, but from a process, often precipitated by "agents of change". The question is not who stimulated the process, but who propels it. Similarly, the basic question to be asked of the agent of change is not what is his social class but where his commitment lies. In the process of catalyzing the people's aspirations into a movement for justice, however, a vanguard of leaders must emerge, and decision-making processes must be established that allow the fullest participation of all." (*To Break the Chains of Oppression*, p. 52, *op. cit.*)

> "Articulating the needs is a complicated process for a community. However, if any coherence of objectives and actions is to be achieved, the articulation of needs is not enough. In fact, "the needs of the people" can easily be manipulated and coopted by the system. The people can only safeguard against the manipulation if they are organized effectively. Organization is not just a means of backing-up a lobbying process. It is essential for the people to identify and articulate a particular demand in a politically relevant way. To do this, people must be organized in order both to act as a political force and to protect themselves against repressive measures by those who oppose change. Repression is always likely. But while an individual is easily eliminated, a group can deal with repression, sometimes even creatively. This does not mean that people's organization in itself is a panacea to tackle the question of power and repression. But it is a necessary step in the struggle for justice and liberation." (*To Break the Chains of Oppression*, p. 54, *op. cit.*)

As CCPD wants to participate and support the struggle of the organized poor and oppressed, a problem that has to be analyzed is alliances and coalitions. Charles Elliot and Françoise de Morsier conclude their book saying:

> "It follows from all we have said that in our view the most creative way forward is not through "poverty planning", ...but rather, through the enablement of the excluded (most immediately through their leadership and their bourgeois allies) to see for themselves the nature of the system in which they are caught and the ways in which that system can be used for their ultimate advantage." (*Patterns of Poverty in the Third World*, p. 399, *op. cit.*)

> "But it must be immediately stated that the orientation of joint action between the poor and the "enlightened bourgeoisie" should be always given by the poor." (*Patterns of Poverty in the Third World*, pp. 395-396, *op. cit.*)

III. An attempt at theological understanding of the struggle of the poor

1. *a)* In the Old Testament, there are six main words to describe the poor. An analysis of that vocabulary indicates a concept of poverty which is different from ours. Today's definition of poverty, as in the Greek and Latin languages, is an absence of goods: it is an economic concept. It is true that the Hebrew language indicates sometimes poverty as an absence (râsh), or as a demand ('ebyôn), but it describes through these words a situation of dependency above all (cf. especially other words: 'ânî; 'ânâw; miskén) or of weakness and powerlessness (dal). For the human beings of the Old Testament, the poor is not so much an indigent but rather someone who is inferior, a lesser person, an oppressed one: *it is then a social concept*. It is perhaps because of this that the poor have looked for the spiritualization of their condition: poverty should not be seen, however, as an ideal of indifference towards the goods of this world, but rather as a sign of willing submission to God's design in love.

b) In the *New Testament*, the poor are not seen as heroes but rather as victims of injustice and oppression. Poverty, in the New Testament, is not presented as something which calls upon people to be generous, nor as an ideal that should be achieved. Basically, it is understood as *an evil* whose victims should be relieved from their pain and suffering. Because the poor are victims of injustice, God in Christ has made an option for them:

the poor will inherit the Kingdom! Translated into action for the communities of the Early Church, this meant that the believers were not pushed to become poor, but rather to see that everybody should have what they need. However, to be more precise, we can say that in the teachings of Jesus we find three lines that are indicating to the people of God that richness should not be pursued by one who wants to be a true disciple of Christ. The first we find in Jesus' criticism of wealth and richness (Luke 12 : 16-21); the second is described in the words with which Jesus portrays the personality of the citizen of the Kingdom of God in the passage which begins the Sermon on the Mount with the "blessings" (Matt. 5 : 3-12): they indicate that those who will be accepted in the Kingdom of God have gone through a life of humility and poverty, but not of power and wealth. The third line is present in the challenge of Christ to make an option between God and Mammon (Matt. 6 : 24; Luke 16 : 23). There is no room for the rich in the Kingdom of God! None who cares for his/her property more than for the commandment of Christ is worthy to be called his disciple!

2. But what do the poor want? What are they expecting? Basically, the manifestation of the Kingdom. But in the meantime, they are striving for a society which could be more comparable with the idea that the Old Testament prophets have given of the messianic realization. One of the main indications of this society (which we mention here because it was indicated by Jesus at the beginning of his ministry according to Luke 4 : 17-21) was the notion of the "Year of Jubilee" (cf. Lev. 25), which never materialized in Israel's history, but which was an indication of the kind of expectations of the 'ânâwi: to be liberated of the fetters of injustice which kept them in situations of poverty and oppression. In a sense, what was proposed in Leviticus 25 was more than a liberating event: it was a programme of structural changes at the economic and social and political levels of the people of Israel. When Jesus mentioned that He had come to make concrete the "acceptable year of the Lord" (Luke 4 : 19), He was indicating that his mission was to incarnate the hopes of the 'ânâwi and the *dal* of Israel, those who are oppressed and live in dependency because of their weakness and powerlessness. Because their hope was not in themselves but in the powerful arm of God, who "has put down the mighty from their thrones and exalted those

of low degree, He has filled the hungry with good things and the rich He has sent empty away" (Luke 1 : 52-53).

Hence the poor, according to the Scriptures, were united in the expectations of the Kingdom that comes, when prevailing oppressive structures will be reversed. Because of this expectation, as a sign of the new things to come and as a concrete manifestation of the will of the members of the Early Church, to confront the evil of poverty, in the community of Jerusalem all were:

> "of one heart and soul, and no one said that any of the things which he possessed was his own, but they had everything in common. And with great power the apostles gave their testimony to the resurrection of the Lord Jesus, and great grace was upon them all. There was not a needy person among them, for as many as were possessors of lands or houses sold them, and brought the proceeds of what was sold and laid it at the apostles' feet; and distribution was made to each as any had need" (Acts 4 : 32-35).

The expectation of a new society implies a certain vision of it, but already now the exercise of actions and programmes which indicate what the poor are aiming at. Charity is of no value in itself, but is valuable in some cases as an indication of relationships that will be established when the messianic Kingdom is accomplished.

3. *What does it mean to the churches today ?* Here, it is appropriate to quote what was stated at the second Montreux Consultation, December 1974, on "Justice and Development":

> "The poor are not yet filled with good things, and the mighty still seem to be on their multinational thrones, though not all too comfortable. The poor are heeding the trumpet and awakening to the call to struggle. The Lord's words in the Synagogue at Nazareth that He has been anointed to bring good news to the poor and to proclaim liberty to the captives ring true with new meaning today. The righteousness of God in the Old Testament has shown itself in the deliverance of the poor from their oppressors, in the vindication of the defenceless, in the protection of the orphan and the widow, in a definite taking of sides with the victims of injustice. Jesus Christ reveals the righteousness of God also in this partisanship with the poor, and we need to ask the ecclesiological question whether the Church can be the Church if it is not identified with the poor. Some would go even further

and insist that the Church has to *be* poor in order to be identified with the poor, and that in a church that is wealthy and powerful the Word of God may be bound. Has a church the right even to assist the poor when it is allied with the oppressor? How can its proclamation then be good news to the poor? What value has its development assistance if its partisanship is with the powerful and the affluent? How can a church that is in servitude to the structures of captivity that belong to the old age be liberated to proclaim the word of liberation and be a true servant of the poor and oppressed?" (*The Ecumenical Review*, Vol XXVII No. 1, January 1975, p. 45).

"How does the Church struggle for its own liberation in order that it may be free to proclaim the gospel of liberation? The struggle for the Church goes on within the Church. The Church, called to be herald, sign, sacrament and agent of the Kingdom, waits for her own liberation by the power of the New Age. What are the elements in this liberation of the Church which will also give free course in the world to the saving Word of God?

a) *The call to repentance:* The churches' repentance can take many forms, depending on the situation and heritage of each. For some rich and powerful churches, repentance and self-emptying may mean the renunciation of wealth and power, a decidedly costly process. Churches would themselves have to know powerlessness in order to be open to the powers of the New Age. To break the alliance with the structures of power may mean the accusation of treason and the possibility of persecution.

b) *The call to defend the defenceless:* This may mean coming to the defence of the dispossessed, fighting for victims of torture, exposing the schemes of those in power, being a voice for the voiceless, confronting the mighty in their insolence, risking our own security and comfort — all at great cost.

c) *Prophetic criticism of the oppressor and proclamation of hope to the poor:* Prophetic criticism may be more than verbal. Sometimes, it may entail treason when measured by the canons of patriotism. The message of salvation may have to aim at the destruction of the structures of oppression and the setting of the captives at liberty. Proclamation that denounces oppression and generates hope may even divide the community of Christians, but Jesus has said also that He has come to bring the sword, not peace. The ambiguity of the Church, in its partial compromise and partial faithfulness, will come to light only with the authentic proclamation of the Word.

d) *A place for the poor to organize their struggle:* Can the Church be a home in all countries for the poor to get together and organize their own struggle? Can the community of the faithful be a place where the poor and the dispossessed can find hospitality, as they used to do in the early days of the Church — not just to be fed and housed, but also to organize themselves for their own emancipation?

e) *The priestly role of intercession and prayer for the poor and the oppressed:* A church that struggles for its own authenticity should also be a priestly community continually lifting up the poor and the oppressed in their prayer and intercession.

The above is not meant to be a list of all the things that the Church is or does. Much of our traditional proclamation, diakonia and education may have to go on. The Church, even as a society, will always remain ambiguous, partly compromised and partly faithful. But the way to authenticity and freedom lies through the cross of redemptive suffering, through repentance and faith, through exposing ourselves in the vulnerability of powerlessness and love." (*The Ecumenical Review*, Vol. XXVII, No. 1, January 1975, p. 46).

Index of Biblical References

Other Orbis books . . .

THE MEANING OF MISSION

José Comblin

"This very readable book has made me think, and I feel it will be useful for anyone dealing with their Christian role of mission and evangelism." *New Review of Books and Religion*
ISBN 0-88344-304-X CIP   *Cloth $6.95*

THE GOSPEL OF PEACE AND JUSTICE

Catholic Social Teaching Since Pope John

Presented by Joseph Gremillion

"Especially valuable as a resource. The book brings together 22 documents containing the developing social teaching of the church from *Mater et Magistra* to Pope Paul's 1975 *Peace Day Message on Reconciliation.* I watched the intellectual excitement of students who used Gremillion's book in a justice and peace course I taught last summer, as they discovered a body of teaching on the issues they had defined as relevant. To read Gremillion's overview and prospectus, a meaty introductory essay of some 140 pages, is to be guided through the sea of social teaching by a remarkably adept navigator."
National Catholic Reporter

"An authoritative guide and study aid for concerned Catholics and others." *Library Journal*
ISBN 0-88344-165-9   *Cloth $15.95*
ISBN 0-88344-166-7   *Paper $8.95*

THEOLOGY IN THE AMERICAS

Papers of the 1975 Detroit Conference

Edited by Sergio Torres and John Eagleson

"A pathbreaking book from and about a pathbreaking theological conference, *Theology in the Americas* makes a major contribution to ecumenical theology, Christian social ethics and liberation movements in dialogue." *Fellowship*
ISBN 0-88344-479-8 CIP   *Cloth $12.95*
ISBN 0-88344-476-3   *Paper $5.95*

CHRISTIANS, POLITICS
AND VIOLENT REVOLUTION

J.G. Davies

"Davies argues that violence and revolution are on the agenda the world presents to the Church and that consequently the Church must reflect on such problems. This is a first-rate presentation, with Davies examining the question from every conceivable angle."

National Catholic News Service
ISBN 0-88344-061-X   *Paper $4.95*

CHRISTIAN POLITICAL THEOLOGY
A MARXIAN GUIDE

Joseph Petulla

"Petulla presents a fresh look at Marxian thought for the benefit of Catholic theologians in the light of the interest in this subject which was spurred by Vatican II, which saw the need for new relationships with men of all political positions." *Journal of Economic Literature*
ISBN 0-88344-060-1   *Paper $4.95*

THE NEW CREATION:
MARXIST AND CHRISTIAN?

José María González-Ruiz

"A worthy book for lively discussion."

The New Review of Books and Religion
ISBN 0-88344-327-9 CIP   *Cloth $6.95*

CHRISTIANS AND SOCIALISM

Documentation of the Christians for
Socialism Movement in Latin America

Edited by John Eagleson

"Compelling in its clear presentation of the issue of Christian commitment in a revolutionary world." *The Review of Books and Religion*
ISBN 0-88344-058-X   *Paper $4.95*

THE CHURCH AND
THIRD WORLD REVOLUTION

Pierre Bigo

"Heavily documented, provocative yet reasonable, this is a testament, demanding but impressive." *Publishers Weekly*
ISBN 0-88344-071-7 CIP   *Cloth $8.95*
ISBN 0-88344-072-5   *Paper $4.95*

WHY IS THE THIRD WORLD POOR?

Piero Gheddo

"An excellent handbook on the Christian understanding of the development process. Gheddo looks at both the internal and external causes of underdevelopment and how Christians can involve themselves in helping the third world." *Provident Book Finder*
ISBN 0-88344-757-6   *Paper $4.95*

POLITICS AND SOCIETY
IN THE THIRD WORLD

Jean-Yves Calvez

"This frank treatment of economic and cultural problems in developing nations suggests the need for constant multiple attacks on the many fronts that produce problems in the human situation."

The Christian Century
ISBN 0-88344-389-9   *Cloth $6.95*

A THEOLOGY OF LIBERATION

Gustavo Gutiérrez

"The movement's most influential text." *Time*

"The most complete presentation thus far available to English readers of the provocative theology emerging from the Latin American Church." *Theological Studies*

"North Americans as well as Latin Americans will find so many challenges and daring insights that they will, I suggest, rate this book one of the best of its kind ever written." *America*
ISBN 0-88344-477-1   *Cloth $7.95*
ISBN 0-88344-478-X   *Paper $4.95*

THEOLOGY FOR A NOMAD CHURCH

Hugo Assmann

"A new challenge to contemporary theology which attempts to show that the theology of liberation is not just a fad, but a new political dimension which touches every aspect of Christian existence."

Publishers Weekly

ISBN 0-88344-493-3   *Cloth $7.95*
ISBN 0-88344-494-1   *Paper $4.95*

FREEDOM MADE FLESH

The Mission of Christ and His Church

Ignacio Ellacuría

"Ellacuría's main thesis is that God's saving message and revelation are historical, that is, that the proclamation of the gospel message must possess the same historical character that revelation and salvation history do and that, for this reason, it must be carried out in history and in a historical way." *Cross and Crown*

ISBN 0-88344-140-3   *Cloth $8.95*
ISBN 0-88344-141-1   *Paper $4.95*

THE LIBERATION OF THEOLOGY

Juan Luis Segundo

"It is a remarkable book in terms of its boldness in confronting the shortcomings of the Christian tradition and in terms of the clarity of vision provided by the hermeneutic of liberation. Segundo writes with ease whether dealing with the sociological, theological, or political roots of liberation. His is a significant addition to the recent work of Cone, Alves, Moltmann, and Gutiérrez because it compels the movement to interrogate its own theological foundations. A necessary addition, in one of the more fruitful directions of contemporary theology, it is appropriate for graduate, undergraduate, or clerical readers." *Choice*

"The book makes for exciting reading and should not be missing in any theological library." *Library Journal*

ISBN 0-88344-285-X CIP   *Cloth $10.95*
ISBN 0-88344-286-8   *Paper $6.95*

MARX AND THE BIBLE

José Miranda

"An inescapable book which raises more questions than it answers, which will satisfy few of us, but will not let us rest easily again. It is an attempt to utilize the best tradition of Scripture scholarship to understand the text when it is set in a context of human need and misery."

Walter Brueggemann, in Interpretation

ISBN 0-88344-306-6   *Cloth $8.95*
ISBN 0-88344-307-4   *Paper $4.95*

BEING AND THE MESSIAH

The Message of Saint John

José Miranda

"This book could become the catalyst of a new debate on the Fourth Gospel. Johannine scholarship will hotly debate the 'terrifyingly revolutionary thesis that this world of contempt and oppression can be changed into a world of complete selflessness and unrestricted mutual assistance.' Cast in the framework of an analysis of contemporary philosophy, the volume will prove a classic of Latin American theology." *Frederick Herzog, Duke University Divinity School*

ISBN 0-88344-027-X CIP   *Cloth $8.95*
ISBN 0-88344-028-8   *Paper $4.95*

THE GOSPEL IN SOLENTINAME

Ernesto Cardenal

"Upon reading this book, I want to do so many things—burn all my other books which at best seem like hay, soggy with mildew. I now know who (not what) is the church and how to celebrate church in the eucharist. The dialogues are intense, profound, radical. *The Gospel in Solentiname* calls us home."

Carroll Stuhlmueller, National Catholic Reporter

ISBN 0-88344-168-3   *Vol. 1 Cloth $6.95*
ISBN 0-88344-170-5   *Vol. 1 Paper $4.95*
ISBN 0-88344-167-5   *Vol. 2 Cloth $6.95*

THE CHURCH AND POWER IN BRAZIL

Charles Antoine

"This is a book which should serve as a basis of discussion and further study by all who are interested in the relationship of the Church to contemporary governments, and all who believe that the Church has a vital role to play in the quest for social justice." *Worldmission*
ISBN 0-88344-062-8   *Paper $4.95*

HISTORY AND
THE THEOLOGY OF LIBERATION

Enrique Dussel

"The book is easy reading. It is a brilliant study of what may well be or should be the future course of theological methodology."
Religious Media Today
ISBN 0-88344-179-9   *Cloth $8.95*
ISBN 0-88344-180-2   *Paper $4.95*

DOM HELDER CAMARA

José de Broucker

"De Broucker, an internationally recognized journalist, develops a portrait, at once intimate, comprehensive and sympathetic, of the Archbishop of Olinda and Recife, Brazil, whose championship of political and economic justice for the hungry, unorganized masses of his country and all Latin America has aroused world attention."
America
ISBN 0-88344-099-7   *Cloth $6.95*

THE DESERT IS FERTILE

Dom Helder Camara

"Camara's brief essays and poems are arresting for their simplicity and depth of vision, and are encouraging because of the realistic yet quietly hopeful tone with which they argue for sustained action toward global justice." *Commonweal*
ISBN 0-88344-078-4   *Cloth $3.95*

LOVE AND STRUGGLE
IN MAO'S THOUGHT

Raymond L. Whitehead

"Mao's thoughts have forced Whitehead to reassess his own philosophy and to find himself more fully as a Christian. His well documented and meticulously expounded philosophy of Mao's love and struggle-thought might do as much for many a searching reader." *Prairie Messenger*

ISBN 0-88344-289-2 CIP   *Cloth $8.95*
ISBN 0-88344-290-6   *Paper $3.95*

WATERBUFFALO THEOLOGY

Kosuke Koyama

"This book with its vivid metaphors, fresh imagination and creative symbolism is a 'must' for anyone desiring to gain a glimpse into the Asian mind." *Evangelical Missions Quarterly*

ISBN 0-88344-702-9   *Paper $4.95*

ASIAN VOICES
IN CHRISTIAN THEOLOGY

Edited by Gerald H. Anderson

"A basic sourcebook for anyone interested in the state of Protestant theology in Asia today. I am aware of no other book in English that treats this matter more completely." *National Catholic Reporter*

ISBN 0-88344-017-2   *Cloth $15.00*
ISBN 0-88344-016-4   *Paper $7.95*

FAREWELL TO INNOCENCE

Allan Boesak

"This is an extremely helpful book. The treatment of the themes of power, liberation, and reconciliation is precise, original, and Biblically-rooted. Dr. Boesak has done much to advance the discussion, and no one who is interested in these matters can afford to ignore his important contribution." *Richard J. Mouw, Calvin College*

ISBN 0-88344-130-6 CIP   *Cloth $4.95*

THE PATRIOT'S BIBLE

Edited by John Eagleson and Philip Scharper

"Following the terms of the Declaration of Independence and the U.S. Constitution, this faithful paperback relates quotes from the Bible and from past and present Americans 'to advance the kingdom and further our unfinished revolution.' " *A.D.*
ISBN 0-88344-377-5   *Paper $3.95*

THE RADICAL BIBLE

Adapted by John Eagleson and Philip Scharper

"I know no book of meditations I could recommend with more confidence to learned and unlearned alike." *St. Anthony Messenger*
ISBN 0-88344-425-9   *Cloth $3.95*
ISBN 0-88344-426-7   *Pocketsize, paper $1.95*

THE LAW AND THE POOR

Frank Parker, S.J.

"This interesting and extraordinarily practical book shows how to make the laws work for the poor rather than against them." *Choice*
ISBN 0-88344-276-0   *Paper $4.95*

DEVELOPMENT: LESSONS FOR THE FUTURE

Thomas Melady and Robert Suhartono

"This volume is written in clear and readable English, with a minimum of professional jargon. It should be of interest to both professionals and interested laymen." *Journal of Economic Literature*
ISBN 0-88344-079-2   *Cloth $6.95*

THE ASSAULT ON AUTHORITY

William W. Meissner

"This is a sober study of authority from a socio-psychological perspective, with strong emphasis on problems of the religious community." *The Critic*
ISBN 0-88344-018-0   *Cloth $7.95*